Paternoster Pocket Books, No. 14

Living Churches

In this book, John Williams does not deal only with the character and calling of the Church of God—there are books enough and to spare that do that—but goes on to examine what was built or that foundation, and in particular to emphasize the vital importance of local leadership and ministry.

Mr. Williams makes a strong plea that the responsibilities of eldership and diaconate service in local churches should be taken much more seriously than they usually are, that definite training for the better fulfilment of such ministries should be undertaken, and that in particular the basic needs of regular, consecutive exposition of the Word of God, and a pastoral ministry throughout the church, should be met, not in a haphazard way as so often obtains at present, but as an essential ingredient of the continuing life and growth of a local "living church".

OTHER TITLES IN THIS SERIES:

THE "JESUS FAMILY" IN COMMUNIST CHINA
D. Vaughan Rees
THE BIBLE AND MODERN MEDICINE
A. Rendle Short
STEEP ASCENT
Dorothy Dennison
THE ADVENTURES OF A DESERTER
Jan Overduin
BY WHAT AUTHORITY?
Bruce Shelley
WHAT ABOUT TONGUE-SPEAKING?
A. A. Hoekema
THE MYSTERY OF ISRAEL
H. L. Ellison
PHYSICIAN HEAL THYSELF
Dorothy Dennison
BLACK AND FREE
Tom Skinner
WORDS OF REVOLUTION
Tom Skinner
HOME BIBLE STUDIES
Derek Copley
HOLY SPIRIT BAPTISM
A. A. Hoekema
CHRISTIAN SCIENCE
A. A. Hoekema
JEHOVAH'S WITNESSES
A. A. Hoekema
MORMONISM
A. A. Hoekema
SEVENTH-DAY ADVENTISM
A. A. Hoekema

LIVING
CHURCHES

*A Reconsideration of their
Basis of Life and Leadership*

John Williams, B.D., M.Th., A.L.B.C.

EXETER
THE PATERNOSTER PRESS LTD.

AUSTRALIA:
Emu Book Agencies Pty., Ltd.,
63, Berry Street, Granville 2142, N.S.W.

SOUTH AFRICA:
Oxford University Press,
P.O. Box 1141, Oxford House,
11 Buitencingle Street, Cape Town

Made and Printed in Great Britain for
The Paternoster Press Ltd Paternoster House
3 Mount Radford Crescent Exeter Devon
by A Wheaton & Co Exeter

Contents

Preface   7

Part I: Life-Patterns in the Churches

1 *Basic Doctrines*   11

2 *The New Testament Pattern*   26

3 *The Assembly in Practice*   35

4 *Establishing Indigenous Churches*   47

Part II: Leadership in the Churches

5 *Eldership in the New Testament*   57

6 *The Character and Ministry of Elders*   70

7 *The Recognition and Training of Elders*   84

Part III: Ministry and Service in the Churches

8 *Declaring the Whole Counsel of God*   95

9 *The Pastoral Ministry*   102

10 *Deacons in the New Testament*   117

11 *The Character, Ministry and Encouragement of Deacons*   125

Bibliography   141

TO

MY WIFE

THROUGH WHOSE PATIENCE
UNDERSTANDING, HELP AND LOVE
I AM CONSTANTLY
ENCOURAGED

Preface

LIVING AS WE DO IN AN AGE OF DISSENT, IN WHICH established institutions and traditions are suspect, as Christians we are tempted to adopt one of two options. On the one hand we may elect to join hands with some vociferous minority and seek in iconoclastic fervour to destroy the "establishment" (whatever that is!). On the other, we may decide to follow the safe, majority policy, settle more deeply into our rut, and stolidly determine to protect all that tradition which we believe is sacrosanct. There is, of course, another sterile option known as "unconcerned uninvolvement," but that is practically unchristian.

In ecclesiastical matters as in others, everything is "up for grabs," colloquially speaking, and whatever our reaction or option we ought to be glad of the opportunity for discussion. If our church polity is being assailed there is no need to run away and hide. Let us rather stay and be glad of the opportunity to talk scripturally about the possibilities that are before us. To come to the heart of the matter : there are today many people who have had a surfeit of denominationalism and the established churches with their intricate liturgies, their top-heavy bureaucracy and sundry archaisms. They feel that our crying need is to break through the crust of tradition and find the heart of our faith. Now this is surely commendable. We ought to be willing humbly to inquire into the Word of God, to abandon all that tradition we find to be expendable, and then positively to give fresh and meaningful expression to "the faith once delivered to the saints."

However, it seems that unless we keep before us the importance of the Church which is the body of Christ, particularly as it is visibly and vitally expressed in this or that local church, there is the danger of our missing God's

7

best in terms of fruitful Christian fellowship. No matter how exciting the advertised attractions of the extra-Church organization, we do well to recall that most heartening promise of the Lord Jesus, "For where two or three are gathered in my name, there am I in the midst of them" (Matt. 18:20). Where Christ is present and His authority acknowledged, the possibilities are still boundless.

Most of these chapters have appeared as magazine articles and I am grateful to readers, friends, and in particular the publisher, who have encouraged me to give this material a more permanent form. It is my hope that these pages written in the midst of a busy life of preaching, counselling, and seeking to share with other elders the work of shepherding "the flock of God", may help stimulate Christians, young and old, to a deeper concern and more active involvement in the life of a local church.

If by reason of our frequent reference to the "Brethren Movement", so-called, we are accused of bias, then we must accept the charge. However, let us hasten to say in defence that we refer to this movement not because we revere its traditions, but because the principles it has stressed do under God give opportunity for a free expression in any generation or society of New Testament Christianity. Here if you will is a living option, relevant even in a space-age.

Our prayer is that we, "speaking the truth in love, may grow up in all things into him, which is the head, even Christ; from whom all the body fitly framed and knit together through that which every joint supplieth, according to working in due measure of each several part, maketh the increase of the body unto the building up of itself in love" (Eph. 4:15-16).

JOHN WILLIAMS

Victoria, B.C., 1970.

Part I

Life-Patterns in the Churches

"And the glory of the Lord came into the house by the way of the gate whose prospect is toward the east. And the spirit took me up, and brought me into the inner court; and behold, the glory of the Lord filled the house. And I heard one speaking unto me out of the house; and a man stood by me. And he said unto me, Son of man, this is the place of my throne, and the place of the soles of my feet, where I will dwell in the midst of the children of Israel for ever" (Ezek. 43:4-7).

One

Basic Doctrines

> *"For as the body is one, and hath many members, and all the members of the body, being many, are one body; so also is Christ. For in one Spirit were we all baptized into one body, whether Jews or Greeks, whether bond or free; and were all made to drink of one Spirit"* (1 Cor. 12:12-13).

IN THESE EARLY CHAPTERS WE SHALL ATTEMPT TO present what we believe are the distinctive contributions to the contemporary witness of the Christian Church offered by those known as "Brethren." At the outset it will be necessary to point out that since local churches or "assemblies" of Brethren are independent and autonomous, it is difficult to generalize or treat them as a denomination in the usual sense of the word. However, since for practical purposes these assemblies are usually distinctive and identifiable, and since in this context we are attempting to underline and state positively for the benefit of our fellow-Christians what, if any, are the distinctive contributions Brethren have to make, we must be allowed some broad generalizations. If this or that "distinctive emphasis" seems quite neglected in any particular assembly of Christian Brethren known to our readers, we would point out two things. First, exceptions prove the rule; and second, vital organisms are notoriously nonconformist!

Having issued this apology and warning, we shall seek to

demonstrate that the following represent not only things distinctive of the Brethren movement but a valid, as well as valuable, contribution to the life and witness of the Christian Church today. Perhaps it will help to underline the importance of our subject, if we note that only if the assemblies have such a valid witness have they a real reason for existence in this age of religious fragmentation. There is no point in perpetuating anything that resembles uncalled-for division or protest.

The following then, are some of the distinctive emphases made by Brethren.

1. The Scriptures are final, peerless and authoritative, not only in matters of personal faith and practice but in patterns of corporate worship and local church procedures.

2. Christ is not only acknowledged, but recognized practically as the pre-eminent Lord and Head of the assembly.

3. As there is only one Lord Jesus Christ, who is the Head, so there is one mystical body : His church, of which every regenerate person is a member. This oneness of the body of Christ is to be demonstrated and never obscured by each local church.

4. New Testament churches are independent and autonomous.

5. The original simplicity of New Testament ecclesiology is as practicable and applicable today as ever.

6. The doctrine of the priesthood of all believers must be given practical and cogent expression in the life and worship of the church.

7. The Lord's Supper is to be given a central place in the life of the church as an occasion of remembrance of the Lord Jesus, a time for worship and spiritual renewal, and an opportunity to give visible expression to the central truths of Christianity.

8. Local churches are committed to a programme of spiritual proliferation by means of corporate and personal evangelism, and missionary enterprise both at home and overseas.

The Authority of Holy Scripture

Today there is considerable discussion as to the ground of authority. Some find their authority in reason, others in the Church, and others in the Bible as the Word of God. Among the last, Brethren may humbly claim a unique place. They claim to make it their undeviating practice to test not only their personal beliefs and manners by Holy Scripture, but also their corporate teachings and particularly their church procedures.

It might be argued that Evangelicals as a whole stand for the unsuperseded authority of Scripture. While this may be true, no "denomination" accepts the Bible as its *only* pattern for church polity and practice in quite the same way as the Christian Brethren. Wherever you find a Brethren assembly, whether they accept such a name or not, you will find a group committed to New Testament ecclesiology, at least in theory. They will not question the plenary inspiration of Scripture. Indeed, they would probably be prepared to take up the cudgels with anyone who did.

Critics of the Brethren have sometimes accused them of over-emphasizing the letter of Scripture at the expense of its spirit, and this criticism has, unfortunately, often been valid. However, even this mistake has been made in all good faith, at least as far as the integrity of Scripture is concerned. We are not here discussing Brethren interpretation of Scripture, but rather emphasizing the central and unchallenged place that the Bible holds among them. We believe that it is this total commitment to the authority of Scripture which has preserved the Brethren from the ravages of modernism. Further, it should be noted that their submission to the authority of Scripture is an evidence of their submission to Christ, who not only taught His followers to obey the Scriptures, but obeyed them Himself.

The following words of Henry Craik, a teacher and writer associated with the Brethren Movement in its early days, well illustrate this position in relation to Scripture :

What we mean by the authority of the Bible, is the authority of the Bible when rightly read, correctly translated, and judiciously expounded and applied. Its teachings when thus elicited, are to be received with the most entire deference.[1]

In a similar vein, another of the early Brethren, Henry Borlase, wrote :

The fundamental Protestant rule should lead us, in common consistency, to refer to the Scriptures, not only for that which ministers to the edification of individuals, but for the form of ecclesiastical polity which God Himself has revealed in His Word, which in its general principles, unless unanimity be not a duty in the church of Christ, must be there fully and distinctly exhibited. . . . But when this declaration is restricted, on the one side by formularies constructed as terms of communion, and on the other by systems of church government devised by man and accommodated to the circumstances of time and place, the state of the Christian Church presents an anomalous appearance, sadly at variance with its profession. In the Word of God however, may be found a complete exemplar of the Divine will, in the inspired constitution of the apostolic churches; and here in perfect order and symmetry exist the rules of government, edification and discipline, devised by Infinite Wisdom, for those who were to be gathered in His name, and builded together for an habitation of God through the Spirit (Ephesians 2:22).[2]

This second quotation makes a particularly "Brethren" emphasis, when it states that the Scriptures should be referred to "not only for that which ministers to the edification of individuals, but for . . . ecclesiastical polity."

[1] *The Authority of Scripture Considered in Relation to Christian Union*, 1863, p. 11.
[2] *Reasons for withdrawing from the Ministry of the Established Church*, 1834, pp. 25 f.

A contemporary teacher among Brethren, speaking of the situation as it existed in the eighteen-thirties, writes :

No effort was made to deal with the great Protestant doctrinal statements; they went behind them to the Bible, which they regarded as the sole source of authority for doctrine and practice. In the early days they tended to avoid both the use and writing of commentaries, lest any particular interpretation of Scripture should seem to have been given priority over another. It is notable that they were among the pioneers in producing a more accurate New Testament text and Bible translation than that found in the King James' version. Even though part of their solution may be questionable, they were the first Christian body since the Reformation to take the problem of the Old Testament in the church seriously. Had their example been more widely followed, it may be that some of the worst results of negative Biblical criticism might have been avoided.[1]

It should be noted here, for the record, that S. P. Tregelles, one of the most notable textual critics of the day, was associated with the Brethren in Plymouth. He produced two important and scholarly works with a view to encouraging and helping independent study of the Scriptures. One was his critical text of the Greek New Testament, completed in 1872; and the other an exhaustive concordance of the Old Testament. Although this latter work, known as *The Englishman's Hebrew and Chaldee Concordance of the Old Testament*, was published under the editorial name of G. V. Wigram, another of the early Brethren, the work was done by Tregelles. Wigram himself produced a companion volume : *The Englishman's Greek Concordance of the New Testament*. Mention must also be made in this context of the three excellent Bible translations made by John Nelson Darby, one of the early leaders of the Brethren movement. Darby's translations are known as *The New Translation* (in English); the *Elberfeld*

[1] H. L. Ellison, *The Household Church*, 1967, pp. 14 f.

Version (in German); and the *Pau Version* (in French). He is the only man to produce translations in three different modern languages. Some measure of the accuracy of Darby's English New Testament may be gained from the fact that it was consulted closely by the company which prepared the Revised Version of the New Testament in 1881.

Since we are seeking to underline the contemporary relevance and value of Brethren teaching as contributing to the witness of the church today, at least something should be noted here about their methods of Bible interpretation. Here there is complete liberty and due recognition of all the help and findings of devout evangelical scholarship. Brethren teachers have been well known for their "typical" and allegorical interpretations of Scripture. No doubt this has been very much over-done, and has led some to read into Scripture much that is not there. However, even this somewhat erratic allegorizing and "spiritualizing" can remind other segments of the church that there is much valuable and relevant teaching for Christians in the Old as well as the New Testament. It may well be that in its attempt at a more realistic interpretation of Scripture, evangelical scholarship has overlooked many valid prophetic and "typical" Old Testament passages. As a rule, great stress is laid on teaching the Bible and Biblical doctrine in a Brethren assembly. The contemporary emphasis on the "discussion-group" type of study of Bible books has always been in vogue among Brethren. They usually describe it as a "Bible reading." Brethren lay particular stress on scriptural eschatology, and to them Evangelicalism owes much of its revived interest in Christ's Second Coming. Generally speaking, Brethren would come in the category of futurist in their interpretation of prophecy. However, their general tolerance in this area of doctrinal discussion might well be emulated by some other right-wing Evangelical groups.

RECOGNITION OF THE HEADSHIP OF CHRIST

While Christians generally acknowledge the doctrine of

the Headship of Christ in the Church, the Brethren seek to give practical and distinct expression to this truth in their assemblies. They believe that each local church is ideally a "miniature" representation of the universal Church. That is to say, just as Christ is the "head over all things to the church, which is His Body" (Eph. 1:22-23), so is He the Head of each local church, and is to be recognized practically there as such (for example, by submission to those whom He has set as under-shepherds in the Church). Indeed each local church is to be thought of in its sphere as the body of Christ (Rom. 12:3-5; 1 Cor. 12). This is not interpreted to mean that a local church is spiritually different or divorced from the one true Church. It emphasizes the independence of each local church and its sufficiency as found in Christ alone, its Risen Head.

Brethren teach in accordance with the New Testament that there is a definite relation between the Church, the body, and its representation in this or that locality, between the Church and the churches. They would describe this relationship as organic rather than organizational.

Writing of this Robert Rendall says:

Local assemblies have their existence in God the Father and (in) our Lord Jesus Christ, and while the activities of such assemblies as touching believers' responsibilities in them, are said to be discharged in the Lord (1 Thessalonians 5:12), their actual standing and existence is said to be in Christ Jesus (1 Thessalonians 2:14). They thus in some sense individually represent the church, of which each may be said to be a microcosm. They are severally founded, as was the church at Corinth, upon Christ Himself (1 Corinthians 3:11), and derive their true validity as churches from that fact. In other words, they exist in virtue of a present relationship to Christ.[1]

The Brethren accept the following corollaries of this Christocentric concept of the local church:

[1] *The Church, A Symposium,* p. 23.

(i) Each church is responsible to and representative of Christ.

(ii) No human being is to be regarded as head, or in charge of a local church. (This is not to deny the scripturally recognized pattern of responsible leadership offered by godly elders.)

(iii) All oral and practical ministry in the local church is to be under the direct control of Christ, as its Chief Shepherd.

(iv) Christ as Head will supply each local church, as exercised before Him, with the gifts requisite for the maintenance of its witness and testimony.

(v) Those who give spiritual guidance and leadership in the local church will do so collegiately, as directly responsible to Christ.

(vi) While there should be fellowship between churches, no one church ideally is dependent on, subject to, nor responsible for the decisions of another. Fellowship between independent autonomous churches is to be cultivated, whereas attempts at federation of churches are best avoided.

(vii) Each local church is assured of the real spiritual presence of Christ in the midst.

(viii) The Lordship of Christ will be expressed and exercised by the Holy Spirit through the Scriptures.

(ix) Each church is a "temple" of the Holy Spirit.

(x) Christ is the source, sphere and goal of each local church.

One of the key verses employed by some Brethren to express the concept of the headship of Christ is Matthew 18:20 : "for where two or three are gathered together in my name, there am I in the midst of them." These words, they aver, suggest that the presence of the living Lord Jesus Christ is vouchsafed to even the smallest possible "quorum" of believers. It is interesting to note that in order to establish a Jewish synagogue a ten man quorum was required.

This thought of the headship of Christ in the Church

is, we submit, an important contribution to contemporary Christian thought. Christ is sufficient to meet the needs of each local church in every age including our own. There is no need for all the elaborate denominational apparatus which most Christians regard as essential to efficient ecclesiastical function and witness. The Church today does not need more leaders trained in the latest organizational techniques which they in turn feel obliged to impose on the Church. In fact, churches need dedicated men who will come together and place all their skill, training, time and talent at the feet of the Risen Head, that He may use them in those churches, for His glory. Such a concept may sound strange to the ears of anyone who can think only in terms of "different levels of control," and "structured authority." Leadership, responsibility, discipline, organization and authority there must be in the local church; but all in an atmosphere of "spiritual spontaneity," as each bows in glad recognition of the supreme and unquestioned Lordship of Christ. The recognition of the Headship of Christ in a local church does not rule out the possibility of a pastoral ministry, the recognition of elders and deacons or the proper conduct of assembly affairs, as already observed. In fact it will call for diligent and spiritual research to discover how by these and other means the Lordship of Christ may be made real in the lives of the people of God.

THE ONENESS OF THE BODY OF CHRIST

Brethren lay particular emphasis on the practical expression of the doctrine of the "oneness of the body of Christ." We must confess immediately that while this is the ideal there has been all too little vital and practical expression of it. There is so much truth in the words of Mrs Edward Trotter writing on the Brethren in her book *Undertones of the Nineteenth Century* (1905):

Actual life is full of anomalies; the fact that a handful of men whose name became a byword of narrow and bigoted exclusiveness, gave to the church and to the world a new and enlarged conception, is not the least among them.

If there was one thing for which early Brethren wished to stand, it was for the oneness of the body. Sectarianism and denominational rivalry were rife in the early nineteenth century, and many informed Christians longed to be delivered from such internecine strife. It was the growing conviction that all denominational barriers were artificial and man-made that, humanly speaking, drew the early Brethren together. Men and women from all kinds of denominational and social backgrounds, including many clergymen, rejoiced to come together on the simple basis of "all one in Christ Jesus."

Speaking of this Christian unity in his earlier days, J. N. Darby writes,

Any ground of meeting which does not admit all the members of the body simply as members of Christ, is not the ground of the church of God; and if the gifts of the different members of the body, wherever they are, be not recognized; or if their exercise be not permitted according to the Scriptures; then that gathering where such conditions exist, is not God's assembly, but man's.

In a similar vein George Müller says,

At the present time I consider it a real privilege to number amongst my few friends and correspondents, denominational missionaries, ministers and clergymen who are serving God more faithfully than I do myself and the intercourse with them enables me to see things from a wider angle, using, for the time being at least, another viewpoint.

H. L. Ellison writes again,

For the most part they had only one motive, not only to preach the duty of Christian unity but even more to demonstrate its possibility. While they had to stress certain elements in the New Testament that justified their action, they were far more concerned with those principles that made unity possible, without forcing those that would participate first painfully to work out a new set of principles and doctrines. To that end they made admission to the fellowship dependent on Christian life and not on the acceptance of any theological formulation. The wisdom of this should be self-evident. The stress is thereby laid where it undoubtedly is in the New Testament.[1]

Catholicity is undoubtedly one of the distinct emphases of New Testament ecclesiology. Christians everywhere are regarded as sharing a common life in Christ. This is demonstrated nowhere more eloquently than in the Lord's Supper, concerning which Paul asks the great question, "the bread which we break, is it not the communion of the body of Christ?" (1 Cor. 10:16).

We are not writing a history of the Brethren Movement, but we must surely ask, in the light of these original ideals and desires, what it was that went wrong. Why did a movement which began with universal communion end in some of its aspects in universal excommunication? Briefly speaking, it was because truth rather than life came to be regarded as the basis of fellowship. Instead of receiving people on the basis of common life in Christ, all sorts of doctrinal shibboleths were invented.

The words of Paul are especially plain on this matter. Writing to the Romans he says, "Him that is weak in faith receive ye, but not to doubtful disputations . . . for God hath received him" (Rom. 14:1, 3); "Wherefore receive ye one another, even as Christ also received you, to the glory of God" (Rom. 15:7); and again, "receive her (Phoebe) in the Lord, worthily of the saints" (Rom. 16:2). This whole passage is an appeal for tolerance and understanding. There must ever be love for "my brother for whom Christ died." Personal prejudice and points of doctrine should

[1] *The Household Church*, p. 14.

never be a means of dividing the children of God. They of all men should have learned the art of agreeing to differ, in a spirit of tolerance and Christ-like love. Anthony Norris Groves expresses this thought clearly when, in writing a letter to J. N. Darby in 1836, he says:

> As any system is in its provision narrower or wider than the truth, I either stop short, or go beyond its provisions, but I would infinitely rather bear with all their evils than separate from their good. These were the then principles of our separation and inter-communion; we had resolved never to try to get men to act in uniformity further than they felt in uniformity; neither by frowns, or smiles; and this for one simple reason, that we saw no authority given us from God thus to act.

Great damage has also been done among Brethren by a misinterpretation of the scriptural teaching about separation. Such texts as, "Come ye out from among them and be ye separate" (II Cor. 6:17) have become slogans of narrow-minded men who are inclined to "wrest the Scriptures" to support their preconceived notions and prejudices. These Old Testament words quoted by Paul in his second letter to Corinth relate in their New Testament context to the specific, historical need of the church at Corinth. He was urging their withdrawal from "unbelievers" and those who were flagrantly immoral. He was certainly not advocating believers withdrawing from each other, nor formal, ecclesiastical excommunication. Another text misused by some has been referred to earlier (Matt. 18:20). From this verse the catch phrase "gathered out" has been developed, and then used as if to imply that Brethren have been rescued from the "sects" as a sort of privileged, spiritual élite. Others have pressed this wonderful promise of Christ to mean that only if a local church is "set up" in this or that specific manner can it claim the approval or recognition of Christ. In other words they have manufactured one more sectarian badge, which has nothing more to commend it than all the other denominational tags, unless it be grandiloquence. It reads: "Those gathered in the name of the Lord Jesus."

Writing on this particular point G. C. D. Howley says:

The words of this text have sometimes been misinterpreted and have been regarded, perhaps, almost as a religious slogan, as though to be 'gathered' is a permanent state irrespective of spiritual condition. The late Harold P. Barker once wrote a booklet to show the error of this outlook, and he pointed out that to omit the word 'together' is to misquote the text. To be gathered together in His name means to meet with Christ's authority for our gathering. It means to meet as representing His interests among men. It means to come together as those who reflect, in some measure, the character of our Lord. When men and women who have some likeness to Christ meet together with His authority for so doing, that they may truly represent Him and His interests among their fellows, there, surely, will the gracious promise be fulfilled in power, 'There am I in the midst of them.' There will be a simplicity of spirit and form—of spirit, as Christians who so meet will be free from all bondage in heart and mind; and of form, because they will require nothing of mere externalism to support their life or to keep alive their gatherings.[1]

On this same point C. F. Hogg writes:

We perceive that Matt. 18:20 is among the most heart-searching, awe-inspiring texts in the Scriptures. How often it has been made a shibboleth whereby to identify a party! Should we not rather tremble at such a word? If the Lord is indeed "in the midst" of us, He is there to cleanse His people, calling upon us to put away from ourselves everything that grieves Him: our pride, self-seeking, covetousness, our factions and our strifes and all those "works of the flesh" that mar alike our fellowship with Him and our testimony to the world. If we feel the weight of His Word, if we have any sense of its solemn

[1] *A Return to Simplicity*, p. 16.

reality, we shall come together with humbled hearts that we may escape His judgment by anticipating it.[1]

However far short of the ideal the Brethren Movement has fallen, through personality contests and the like, the doctrine of the oneness of the body of Christ may still be regarded as its raison d'être. We can, if we will, give a revitalised expression to this truth, but it will call for the utmost honesty and courage. Early nineteenth century Brethren were pioneers in expressing it and in this second half of the twentieth century we are called to follow them in so far as they followed the Scriptures. It is a sad commentary on our traditionalism that we Brethren are some of the slowest to extend a gracious hand of fellowship to Christians who do not regularly associate with us. Often a Christian will find a more practical expression of the oneness of the body outside Brethren circles than inside them. This is tragic, and it behoves us to search our hearts and mend our ways. We must put away our sectarian spirit and be willing to call and treat as brethren all whom Christ has received. Obviously this does not mean harbouring heretics and miscreants.

Let us accept the challenge of our day and show ourselves as unquestionably committed to the scriptural position of spiritual union. We must give visible expression to this concept, and if this mean joining hands in testimony with other Christians at the practical and local level, then let us be glad to do it. The idea that we must keep up our fences to prevent fellowship with other fine, Bible-loving Christian groups is entirely foreign to and hateful to God! The fears sometimes expressed, when such whole-hearted fellowship with other Christians is advocated, stem from ignorance and unspiritual convictions. No assembly will lose from expressing Christian grace. Obviously the elders will not suddenly abdicate their God-given responsibilities of guarding and guiding the flock. If we are instructed in the Word of God, which is often our boast, what is there to fear from fellowship with other groups of

[1] *The Church—A Symposium*, p. 210.

God's people? Indeed, if we were more inclusive and a lot less exclusive, others might want to share some of the blessings that are found in our assembly fellowship.

Further, we must expose the sham which will accept oral ministry from *bona fide* Brethren speakers only. This is true sectarianism. How can we honestly refuse the oral ministry of men who are Christ's gifts to the Church? We read their books, we sing their hymns, we listen to sermons which are often little more than a rehash of their commentaries. However, we are told by some that we must never allow these "gifts of the risen Christ" the freedom of our platform. Such glaring inconsistency calls for the most courageous treatment.

We do well to remember Henry Craik's words written in 1863 :

> Meanwhile, let us watch against a self-conceited and superficial dogmatism, and let us ever firmly protest against the assumption of those who, by reason of what they regard as a more Scriptural mode of meeting than that adopted by other Christians, are disposed to arrogate to themselves the high prerogative of being the only church upon earth. Let us cherish the far more comforting and exhilarating conviction that all who truly love the Saviour compose His church and that all such, being united to Him now, shall continue to be united to Him, and to each other throughout the ages of eternity.[1]

On the other hand when we speak of the oneness of the body of Christ it must not be construed that we are advocating linking arms with the religio-political power-structure of contemporary ecumenism. The mystical body of Christ is composed of that company of the redeemed each one of whom is personally linked in the life-union of faith in Christ. They are linked to each other because they are first linked to Christ. This is as different from that conglomeration of religious hybrids known as the ecumenical movement as light is from darkness.

[1] *New Testament Church Order*, p. 30.

Two

The New Testament Pattern

> *"Again I say unto you, that if two of you shall agree on earth as touching anything that they shall ask, it shall be done for them of my Father which is in heaven. For where two or three are gathered together in my name, there am I in the midst of them"* (Matt. 18:19-20).

WHEN BRETHREN SPEAK OF CHRISTIAN SIMPLICITY THEY do not mean childish immaturity, ignorance or imbecility. They mean unpretentiousness, lack of complexity and ornamentation—call it "spiritual ingenuousness," if you will. Lest this sounds negative, let us define "simplicity" in this context as "singleness of purpose" or "Christ-centredness."

It is obvious from reading the New Testament that the primitive church was remarkably simple, in this sense. There were groups of people, sharing a common spiritual life and purpose, unencumbered by extraneous rules and regulations. They breathed the clean, fresh air of the Spirit. They had no official constitutions, registered memberships, elaborate ceremonials, humanly appointed priesthood, but were "all one in Christ Jesus." It was this very simplicity that was their strength, and helped them survive bitter persecution.

Human elements soon spoiled this original outlook. Carnal fear and worldly wisdom demanded sacerdotalism, episcopacy, clerisy, liturgy, and the rest. By the fourth century the Emperor Constantine made Christianity the official state religion. As one writer put it, "He exchanged the glory of God in the church for the pomp and circumstance of the world"! Christendom at large has never recovered from this folly. In spite of this, as church history indicates, attempts have been made through the centuries to recapture the simplicity that was in Christ. It is to one such spontaneous attempt in the early nineteenth century that the Brethren Movement traces its inception.

Simplicity is still a distinctive feature of Brethren assemblies, and it is this desire to conform to the original ideals that disclaims party names and labels. The name "Plymouth Brethren" is quite fortuitous, an accident of history, and the Brethren themselves do not usually wish to accept it. If they have to accept a title or name, for government purposes and the like, they would prefer a less odious and more descriptive one such as "Christian Brethren" or "Open Brethren" (the latter name being used to emphasize their "inclusiveness," as well as to distinguish them from the so-called "Exclusives"). There is, of course, no special virtue in disavowing nomenclature. It was strange logic which caused an acquaintance of the writer's to allow the British Army to register him as "Atheist," rather than "P.B."!

As Patrick Monkhouse, correspondent of the *Evening Standard* noted, when writing of the Brethren:

This is the century of over-organization. Every trade, every art, almost every church is organized, associated, federated; councils and committees multiply; annual conferences meet incessantly to pass resolutions on every subject under the sun. In the midst of these imposing structures, there is one body which has found the secret of vitality in a complete contrary policy. The Brethren Movement—popularly known as the Plymouth Brethren because Plymouth was the first town in England in which it made conspicuous headway—has flourished for more than a hundred years without encrusting itself with the hard shell of hierarchy.[1]

Their emphasis on simplicity must not be construed to mean that Brethren are lacking in order, government, good taste, discipline or even scholarship. They simply refuse to be bound to or by any unnecessary, extra-scriptural paraphernalia. Many Brethren would admit that the idea of informality can be greatly over-done. Indeed it is encouraging to see a growing awareness among Brethren of the desirability of a more carefully planned order of service as well as a more systematic and appealing presentation of the great truths of Scripture. One of the confessed weaknesses of "assemblies", for all their emphasis on the Bible, has been the lack of its orderly, public exposition. This has been due very largely to a phobia about something rather carelessly called a "one-man ministry." In steering away from this spectre, Brethren have all too often allowed any man to preach on any subject, at any time, and in any manner. We must always keep in view those important words of Paul to the Corinthians, "Let all things be done decently and in order" (I Cor. 14:40). There is no excuse for the slovenliness with which some of us have become all too familiar. Informality must never become over-familiarity or, worse, irreverence.

This emphasis on simple informality in worship has on occasion been used to excuse shoddy buildings and slipshod programmes. H. L. Ellison has an amusing paragraph on this. He writes :

Until recently many good Christians seem to have thought that ugliness was next to godliness. The sheer ugliness of many places of worship built in the last century by godly men is incredible. It cannot have been accidental, nor was it necessarily the result of skimping; it must have been the result of deliberate effort. If any-

[1] *Evening Standard*, April 19th, 1937.

one tells me it was a protest against the ornateness and luxury of Roman Catholicism and of the State Church, I have only to point him to many a Friends' Meeting House and early Dissenting chapel, where the utmost plainness contrives to produce the impression of real beauty. Some of our halls are beyond redemption, inside and out. But they can at least be made and kept bright and clean. Attractive paint cannot cost much more than those strange browns and off-greens that seem to have been made specially for some places of worship—at least I have never seen them anywhere else except in the wards of those old municipal infirmaries and workhouses that are gradually becoming a thing of the past.[1]

These things are becoming exceptional and while still maintaining simplicity there are today many beautiful as well as functional buildings being used by Brethren.

We must ask ourselves whether this distinctive emphasis on simplicity is still valid and needed by the church at large. We believe it is. In many circles there is more and more emphasis on aesthetic appeal, ritual, ornateness, ecclesiastical dogmas, and academics. These extras so easily become religious crutches or even substitutes for spiritual reality. It may come as a jolt to good churchmen and traditionalists alike to discover how unpretentious and ordinary Christian churches were in New Testament times. We may attempt to cushion the shock by arguing that while such simplicity was feasible in those distant, un-enlightened times it would not work today. However, the simple fact remains that it does work today. Given fair opportunity this simple, Christ-centred concept is still practicable and, in fact, eminently suited to the spiritual needs of our complex society. Who is to deny that the religious frustration of our contemporaries and their dis-enchantment with what they call "the Church" stem as much from the over-elaborateness and often unintelligible

---

[1] *The Household Church*, p. 31.

format of established Christianity as from their unwillingness to try to understand what it is all about.

The man of today, like the man of Paul's day, needs to be told plainly that he is a sinner and that all God's blessings are freely and directly available to him personally through faith alone. The total context of this message is important if it is to be effective. Worship in this space age does not depend on externals or intermediaries any more than on computers and gadgets. Present-day Christians need reminding that wherever the redeemed assemble under the authority of Christ to preach and witness to the Word of God and observe the simple Christian ordinances, there He is in the midst. Nothing could be more humbling and certainly nothing more stimulating.

THE AUTONOMY OF LOCAL CHURCHES

A significant feature of Brethren teaching is the strong emphasis on the autonomy of local churches. From its inception, the movement has stressed the independence of each congregation. In fact it was the undoing of the "Exclusive Brethren" that they rejected this idea of each local church's direct dependence on the Lord. Their emphasis on federalization meant that minor, local troubles were magnified and caused divisions throughout the entire group of associated churches. In fact, a man's attitude to local and historical issues became so important to the Exclusives that his acceptance or rejection by them depended on how he judged this or that question. The recognition of local church autonomy has the salutary effect of insulating local problems as well as preventing the unchurching of dissenting groups. When churches are strictly affiliated there is a strong danger of accepting as *bona fide* churches only those within the association, and of viewing all outside it with suspicion, even refusing Christian fellowship to their members. Autonomy also makes for greater flexibility and liberty—and here lies one of the secrets of the Brethren Movement's success.

One distinguished teacher among Brethren says:

The apostolic churches were each autonomous, no parent or metropolitan church had any jurisdiction beyond its own borders. Once a local·church was established, it maintained its own life and order without any necessity to refer to other or larger churches. This is not to say that good counsel might not be sought from others, but that no outsiders had any right to interfere in the internal affairs of local churches. The internal sovereignty of churches was thus preserved, and their direct dependence upon the Lord could be maintained. This simple principle has often been found a safeguard to preserve the very life of an assembly of christians. Its out-working historically and in modern times is sufficient evidence of its wisdom.[1]

A local church is a living organism, and as such cannot be hidebound and shackled by regulations. Conformity to any standard or pattern other than Scripture will destroy local church independence and lead to bondage. Commenting on this, as seen historically in the Brethren Movement, Ellison writes :

Partly because they realized that the New Testament teaches the independence of the local church, partly because they saw clearly that denominational splits are made possible by the linking up of like-minded bodies throughout a district or even a country, they insisted on strict independence. No fellowship was entitled to sit in judgment on another. While one group was concerned with unity and saw in the New Testament picture of the church the ideal way of reaching it, the other was far more concerned with correct doctrine, without which they could see no unity. Especially their doctrine of the church drove them to separate themselves from those who did not agree with it. This they did in a spirit of extreme bitterness, asserting that those who could not see eye to eye with them had sinned against the light

[1] G. C. D. Howley in *A Return to Simplicity*, p. 18.

and were, in fact, far worse than those who had not had
the light at all. They followed a path that led them to
increasing divisions and in many cases to extravagances
that have made them the laughing-stock of the popular
press today.[1]

There is never any suggestion of federalization in the New
Testament writings. Paul addresses individual churches,
but never suggests that this or that church has any jurisdiction beyond its own members. It is true that he writes
to the Galatian churches collectively, because there was a
common doctrinal problem confronting all of them. He
also envisages a group of churches combining in some
specific project, such as a collection for the poor Christians
of Judea (I Cor. 16:1; II Cor. 8:19). He speaks of "all the
churches of the saints" (I Cor. 14:33) and of "the churches
of God," but there is never the slightest hint of congrega-
tional affairs being subject to outside decisions. New
Testament Christians belonged to this or that local church,
as they belonged by spiritual birthright to the universal
Church. There was never any idea of their belonging to a
national group of churches, as if in some way distinct from
all others. Geographical place names are never used adjec-
tivally in the New Testament. It is somewhat misleading
even today to speak of the "Corinthian church" or for
that matter the London church, unless by such terms we
mean the aggregate of all believers within that particular
locality. A New Testament church was usually described as
"the church of God at X" or "the saints which are at
Ephesus" or "at Philippi." Paul's words to the Corinthians
are particularly helpful in this regard. He writes, "unto
the church of God which is at Corinth . . . called saints . . .
with all that in every place (literally, "location"; "those
who in any place", Amp.) call upon the name of Jesus
Christ our Lord" (I Cor. 1:2). This verse, as well as
emphasizing the catholicity of Christianity, allows the
possibility of there being several local churches within one

[1] *The Household Church*, p. 16.

metropolitan area, rather than one city church with several branches.

The phrase "church of God" is never applied in the New Testament, to anything bigger than a local church. This is true even of a verse like, "So the church throughout all Judea and Galilee and Samaria had peace, being edified, and walking in the fear of the Lord and in comfort of the Holy Ghost, was multiplied" (Acts 9:31). The singular "church" is not used here (or anywhere else in the New Testament for that matter) in an ecumenical sense. It refers to the members of the Jerusalem church now scattered by persecution. There was hardly time for the formation of churches in all the places to which these Jerusalem Christians were scattered. Once these churches were established they are called in accordance with regular New Testament usage, "the churches (plural) of God which are in Judea" (I Thess. 2:14; Gal. 1:22).

Even in the Apocalyptic vision the seven churches of Asia are named and viewed as independent entities. Christ is seen walking among them, as among seven golden lampstands. It may be of small moment, but it is at least noteworthy in this context that there are seven separate lampstands, not one seven-branched lampstand as in Exodus 25:37.

This other Brethren emphasis represents a vital witness to the church and world of our day. We live in an age of ecumenicity which is witnessing the formation of what one contemporary paper calls "a Protestant-Orthodox Curia".[1] Its tentacles stretch out and threaten to embrace, if not strangle, Christendom. Already its powerful influences are being felt on far-off mission fields as in the homelands. Its ever increasing pressures are applied to produce conformity and compromise. Its loudly proclaimed goals of winning the world and fostering Christian charity need not deceive us. Dr. Eugene Carson Blake, a former President of the Ecumenical Movement puts it this way :

God has opened a great, new door to churches everywhere—a door that uniquely leads to the whole world

[1] *Christianity Today*, March 4, 1966.

in its present need. This door is the Ecumenical Movement. By it Christians can be rescued from their cosy hearths and comfortable household gods and carried out into the wide sea of involvement with God's universal church.[1]

This sounds wonderfully evangelical until we are reminded that the ecumenists are devoted syncretists. Noting this, *East Asia's Millions* says:

Once the validity of this syncretistic principle is granted, the eyes that once looked with tolerance at evangelistic activity now harden to a cold stare. No one has a right to press his religion on others. This means a new problem: organized, ecclesiastical hostility to evangelism, now slandered as 'proselytism'. Daniel T. Niles, another prominent ecumenist, has already impatiently affirmed, 'Proselytism can and ought to be controlled.' Such pontifications posit the existence of an ecclesiastical power structure that can eliminate the unwanted evangelist (or missionary).[2]

In the light of this pressure for unity and conformity, Brethren would point out that, while they believe Christians to be duty bound diligently to "keep the unity of the Spirit in the bond of peace" (Eph. 4:3), Scripture nowhere envisages anything other than spontaneous and spiritual union. God's plan is for autonomous independent, Christocentric churches. These will survive totalitarian pressures, whether from ecclesiastical or political sources. Denominations can be crushed; federalization is doomed to fail; but autonomous Christian churches will survive, as they have throughout the centuries. They are surviving today even in places like Russia, Cuba and Red China. They have no political ambitions, their plan is not to reform society, but to witness humbly by life and lip to Jesus Christ as the Saviour of the world.

---

[1] Sermon as quoted by *East Asia's Millions*, November 1965.
[2] *East Asia's Millions*, November 1965.

Three

The Assembly in Practice

> *"And they continued stedfastly in the apostles' teaching and fellowship, in the breaking of bread and the prayers . . . and day by day continuing stedfastly with one accord in the temple, and breaking bread at home, they did take their food with gladness and singleness of heart, praising God and having favour with all the people. And the Lord added to them (mg. "added together") day by day those that were being saved"* (Acts 2:42, 46-47).

WHILE THE GREAT SCRIPTURAL DOCTRINE OF THE priesthood of all believers is held by all truly evangelical churches, it has received a special notice and emphasis in Brethren circles.

Kirby notes this in his review, *The Protestant Churches of Britain.* He writes:

From the outset the emphasis of the brethren has been emphatically upon the priesthood of all believers. They repudiate any and every form of clericalism and stress that in the local assembly, those called to leadership must be guided by the Holy Spirit" (ch. VII, p. 71).

In order to clarify, we might attempt a brief statement

35

of the doctrine. It says that, whereas under the Old Covenant the priesthood was limited to the chosen family of Aaron, under the New Covenant all believers are priests and have equally and without distinction the privilege of approach to God in worship.

If the Brethren have a particular contribution here, it is in regard to their attempt at a practical implementation of this idea. They believe that it is possible to give a much more visible expression to the doctrine of the priesthood of all believers than is sometimes acceptable, even in the great evangelical churches.

1. They stress the importance of a Spirit-endued, or what might be called in some circles, a "lay" ministry.
2. They stress the centrality of the Lord's Supper and its weekly celebration in the context of an "open" service. (Here, "open" means unarranged and spontaneous.)

Some further explanation of the first of these emphases will be attempted here. We will deal with the second under a separate heading.

SPIRIT-ENDUED MINISTRY

The following note is helpful here :

The Brethren, after the evangelical revival of the 18th Century had again restored the great gospel doctrines to their true position, gathered up these ideals. In addition they took to their logical conclusions the principles of the charismatic ministry (i.e., ministry deriving from the gift given by God, and not from some form of sacramental succession), and the priesthood of all believers.[1]

Brethren strongly contest the generally accepted distinction between the clergy and the laity. They believe and

[1] Excerpt from *Notes on the Brethren Movement*, September 1960, by F. R. Coad.

teach that since all Christians are "priests," it is quite erroneous to pay court to a privileged élite called the "clergy." In practice, all the men and women in a Brethren assembly are viewed as equally privileged before God in worship. There is none more "officially qualified" than others to "lead worship", just as there is no individual person who can act in the capacity of mediator for the rest of the assembly.

This emphasis also affects arrangement and conduct of services in a Brethren assembly. Often a prayer meeting or Bible study will be convened without visible leadership, and this is always true of the service for the breaking of bread. It is quite possible that several men will take part in one meeting. Women are not encouraged to take spoken part in official services of the church where both sexes are participating. This restriction, generally based on the teaching of Paul's epistles (I Tim. 2:8-15; I Cor. 14:34-35), is much less significant and difficult for them than many of the Brethren's critics seem to imagine. Furthermore, they recognize that their women, although silent, are "worshippers" equally with the men. There is not the slightest suggestion of a diminution of the women's privilege in this regard. It is simply a matter of emphasizing the complementary rôles of male and female in the assembly. Brethren usually differentiate between what may be called somewhat tentatively "positional" and "practical" truth. That is, while they recognize that in Christ (positionally) male and female are on equal footing, they see a distinction made in the New Testament between the public, church-function of the male and that of the female. Paul does offer reasons for such discrimination in practice, in his pastoral letters (I Tim. 2:11-14), and the eminent suitability of such an arrangement is manifest even today, if only to prevent the strange excesses permitted in those churches where there is undue female domination. To any who would repudiate such teaching as being based on something which was merely a Pauline emphasis, Brethren would generally reply that for them, as indeed for the apostle Peter

(II Pet. 3:16), the Pauline epistles are "Scripture", and therefore authoritative.

The Brethren do not limit preaching or teaching to an individual or special class of people. All the men who are capable are eligible to participate in any function. This does not mean that anybody is allowed to "hold the floor" at any time. Brethren are great believers in spiritual endue-ment for ministry, and the elders or "overseers" who are the recognized leaders in a local assembly, will see to it that only those equipped for the task are granted the privilege of public ministry. In fact, since these elders view themselves as responsible for the assembly's spiritual well-being under God, they will take definite steps to provide a suitable, spiritual diet so that the Christians are established and edified. More thought is being given given in some forward-looking assemblies today to the matter of public ministry within the limits of New Testament principles. They are, in fact, realizing in some quarters that even a sustained, expository ministry in one location on the part of one, suitably gifted individual (*unum inter pares*) is not in conflict with New Testament principles. Indeed many feel that this is a recovery of the type of ministry recog-nized among the early Brethren as in true New Testament tradition. Some assemblies are also recognizing the value of sponsoring young men in training programmes, so that they may sharpen their God-given gifts for use in full-time Christian service.

Even where a man is responsible for much of the public ministry in an assembly's weekly schedule, it is still clearly taught and expressed that it is the man's God-given gift that makes room for him, not some imaginary, inalienable right, by virtue of his ordination or qualification as a "minister." Speaking of early Brethren practice in this matter Ellison writes :

Ministers, elders and deacons who came to them found that their standing was not challenged, but it was made clear to them that in the new fellowship their position would depend entirely in the quality of their lives and the spiritual gifts they showed. In other words, their leaders were not marked out by human appointment but by the general agreement of the fellowship that they possessed the qualities demanded by the New Testament for elders (bishops) and deacons. In addition it was recognized that some had the gift of teacher, pastor or evangelist. Tremendous stress was laid on the duty of all who possessed any gift to use it and on the duty of the assembly, as they called the local group, to make the use of that gift possible.[1]

While full opportunity is to be given for this Spirit-endued ministry in Brethren circles they will not usually tolerate excess or disorder. They believe, in accordance with Paul's words to the Corinthians, that "the spirits of the prophets are subject to the prophets; for God is not a God of confusion, but of peace; as in all the churches of the saints" (I Cor. 14:32-33). Brethren also recognize that a man may be gifted and called of God to a whole-time ministry as an evangelist or Bible teacher. Such men tend to be itinerant and completely independent, having no guaranteed stipend. These men are said to live by faith or, to use another Brethren phrase, "look to the Lord for their support." The New Testament clearly teaches that "they which proclaim the gospel should live of the gospel" (I Cor. 9:14; cf. whole chapter). It would, however, be a mistake to suppose that the method for supporting the Lord's servants traditionally adopted by Brethren is the only one possible in the light of New Testament teaching. Furthermore, it is possible that this idea of an itinerant ministry has been greatly overdone in Brethren circles. The New Testament also provides for a resident teaching ministry supported by a local church (I Tim. 5:17).

There can be no denying that this emphasis on total personnel involvement is a significant contribution to the contemporary witness of the Christian church. More and

[1] *The Household Church*, p. 15.

more scope is being given to the so-called "laity" in the great denominations today. Ministers are looking for means of stirring their armchair, spoon-fed congregations to action. The answer may well be in the principles stressed by the Brethren in regard to the cultivation and exercise of spiritual gift. We may humbly note that men reared in Brethren circles are often the vanguard in great spiritual and lay evangelistic movements, such as Christian Business Men's Committee International, Gideons, Billy Graham Crusades, Bible Conferences, Scripture Union, Inter-Varsity and such like. This is no proof of spiritual superiority, but rather of the opportunity of development of gift afforded in the assembly set-up. (Of course, it is hoped that a man's involvement in these extra-church activities will in no way diminish his sense of responsibility to his local church, nor his usefulness in it.)

It may be significant, too, that in these days when even in evangelical circles the idea is abroad that we must build bigger and bigger congregations, Brethren assemblies generally divide or "hive off" when they reach about the 150/200 mark. This has a twofold purpose. First it multiplies the places of witness, and second, it stimulates involvement and participation.

Speaking of the doubtful comparative value of a fully itinerant ministry, it is interesting to discover that there are many young men who in response to the Lord's call are diligently preparing themselves for a life of service in the work of Christ. These young men, for the most part keen, spiritually minded, well-taught and equipped to understand and minister the word of God, are wisely questioning traditional methods in the light of Scripture and sanctified common sense. They are coming to the conclusion that they would better invest their life of service for Christ in a given locality or area than travel the length and breadth of the land in costly itinerations. Far from turning their backs on so-called assembly principles many of these young men have a growing conviction about them. They are understandably fed-up with the straight-jacket of sectarianism and are "all-for" the new "lay-emphasis." They are not going to settle for an alternative, human tradition which, for all its commendability in the nineteenth and early twentieth centuries, is practically unworkable today.

Perhaps as never before in the history of the assemblies we are confronted with the golden opportunity to be of service to Christ and the Church and the world about us. Here are young servants of Christ ready and willing to help local outreach and effort. Tragically, so few of us seem to recognize their potential, or at least are willing to do anything practically to tap it. Are we afraid to take up the challenge? Are we so entrenched in our traditional patterns that we have lost our vision and ability to respond? It is little use sitting in our pews of complacency and lamenting the departure of gift from among us. It is dishonest, to say the least, nostalgically to deplore that there are not nowadays men of the Word who are prepared to make the sacrifices their fathers and grandfathers made. There are! The problem is all too often with the fathers and grandfathers!

Thank God for those men of years and understanding who are still men of vision, and who by lip and life seek to stimulate their successors to shoulder the yoke of Christian service. Timothys there will be so long as there are Pauls to guide and encourage! We must accept this responsibility.

Surely it might be feasible to initiate some kind of unofficial Christian Internship Programme. Considerable prayer and thought would be needed but we must grasp the nettle. Where an assembly concerned about its effectiveness and witness enjoys the fellowship and full time ministry of a pastor-teacher, it might do well to invite two or three young men to come and get involved. Let these young men accept the challenge of their faith and learn alongside a more experienced servant of Christ. Through first hand contact with day to day assembly problems and face to face encounters with heart-rending needs and sorrows the young man would be matured and prepared for other fields of service. He would learn to work with people, to take orders instead of giving them. Through careful coaching and guidance in a real-life situation he would soon be ready to launch out and serve in another field of opportunity. It goes without saying there are numerous details to be worked out and questions to be answered, but the need is great, the field is white, the time is now—and there are labourers ready!

We must not dismiss them by saying that a man's gift will make room for him! Quite apart from that being a very doubtful application of a text of Scripture, it just is not true to life that because a man has a gift he will necessarily find a field in which to use it. How does a young man break into a pretty tightly-knit group which, for all its vaunted informality and local church autonomy, has its "list of workers" and *bona-fide* preachers? This is not intended as a criticism of our *modus operandi* (the writer is on the list, through no fault of his own!) it is simply a plea for flexibility and a willingness to be open to receive new ideas and possibilities so that we may share our God-given heritage with others. There are many assemblies prayerfully looking for help from the Lord's servants but they are cautious about inviting a worker who is inexperienced. Unfortunately the inexperienced are those whom we need, not only because through our fellowship and the stimulus of a service-opportunity they may become experienced, but also because they are often youthful and therefore have the ear of their own generation, which we must win for Christ if we are to be true to our trust. It is the responsibility of those of us who are already engaged in service as well as far-sighted assembly elders to look into the exciting possibilities that are before us.

Before concluding this section, a word must be added about the more practical areas of our corporate priesthood. We are inclined to limit what we regard as the Christian's priestly activity to such things as worship and preaching. In fact, Scripture indicates that there is a wide range of "spiritual sacrifices" that a believer-priest can offer, and in so doing win God's approbation. Such things as prayer, the giving of thanks, repentance, doing good, helping the needy and caring for the sick are all priestly acts in this deeper sense (Heb. 13:15-16).

THE CENTRALITY OF THE LORD'S SUPPER

Brethren have always given an important place to the Christian ordinance of the Lord's Supper. It is celebrated by them weekly on the Lord's Day, and is central to all their other assembly activities. Their interpretation of the Supper approximates most nearly to that of Zwingli, who regarded the bread and wine as symbolic only and the partaking of the emblems as a memorial. In an assembly, great stress would normally be laid upon the spiritual presence of Christ at His table, but not in such a way as to suggest that the Lord is more really "present" there than He is, for example, at a prayer meeting or a similar "gathering together in His name."

Brethren generally do not believe that Christ's presence is guaranteed by the bread and wine, nor that He is to be discerned in some quasi-physical sense in these emblems. Indeed, they would be very guarded about describing the Lord's Supper as a "means of grace," except in a relative and secondary sense. Christ's presence, they would say, will be known because Christians are met under His authority, and in obedience to His command.

While remembrance of Christ's sufferings and death will often be the keynote of a service for the breaking of bread, there should always be worship and thanksgiving directed to the risen Christ. It will not be overlooked that our Lord's words at the institution of this Supper were, "This do for a remembrance of me." Everything else will be secondary to, and tending towards, the remembering and honouring of Christ Himself. His glorious Person will, in a sense, take precedence over His saving work, though finally neither can be divorced from the other.

An equally significant thing and something distinctive of Brethren is their manner of conducting what is called in other ecclesiastical circles "the service of Holy Communion." Brethren prefer to call it by its simple, scriptural name, "the breaking of bread." They celebrate the Lord's Supper in the context of an "open" or unarranged service. In this way they believe they can better confess, as well as exercise, their holy privilege of priestly worship. They are particularly sensitive about each believer's responsibility as a member of "a royal priesthood." There will be no presiding minister or elder at such a service, and no one is considered to be more qualified or authorized to dispense the elements than another, since there is nothing priestly nor representative about this act. Each man present is at liberty and is, indeed, encouraged to participate in audible prayer, praise and ministry, to announce a suitable hymn, or even to dispense the bread and wine. Brethren hope that the only restricting of this spontaneity will be by the Holy Spirit. A Christian visitor, unfamiliar with their type of service, will at first be surprised, but more often than not he will go away impressed by its quiet reverence and simple dignity.

Of course we must admit that there is the danger that even the unstructured weekly meeting for the breaking of bread, so dear to Brethren, may develop a liturgy all of its own. It is easy to become wedded to a particular form and way of doing things and mix what is scriptural with what is merely traditional. The important thing to recognize is that the meaningful sharing of the bread and wine as a memorial of Christ is the only part of any communion service which is scriptural in the exact sense. The order of service, its setting, its duration are not prescribed, and for good reason. Valuable and defensible though this or that order of service for communion may be, none is final nor guarantees a deeper experience of the reality of Christ. Spiritual sensitivity and preparation of heart are the vital conditions.

Speaking of visitors, it is noteworthy that the original vision of the Brethren was of an "open" table where all who were true believers in Christ were welcome. This still obtains among Open Brethren (a name generally used to distinguish them from "Exclusive Brethren"). We must note in passing that there are some groups of Brethren, notoriously the so-called "Needed Truth" group formed as a result of a secession in 1893 (and named after their magazine *Needed Truth*), who reject the early principle of communion on the basis of common life in Christ, and substitute for it the principle of "separation". This results in a closed communion in effect, which is of course totally alien to the New Testament. Open Brethren seek to follow the principle stated by Paul : "Wherefore receive ye one another as Christ also received us, to the glory of God" (Rom. 15:7).

Incidentally, while Open Brethren would encourage all Christian believers to be baptized by immersion in accordance with New Testament teaching and precedent, they would not normally consider baptism mandatory for communion nor for church "membership". However, they would be quite likely to suggest to a Christian who continues in regular attendance at The Lord's Supper that he give due consideration to this other ordinance of baptism. Brethren generally aver that, while fellowship in a local church is, like salvation, not dependent on nor effected by baptism, it is clearly associated with it in the New Testament, which nowhere contemplates the idea of an unbaptized believer. (Exclusive Brethren tend to be paedo-baptist, practising what they describe as "household baptism".)

Visitors who are not Christians are welcome to attend The Lord's Supper although they would be discouraged from taking the bread and wine. Sometimes a convenient area will be set aside for visitors to "observe" the breaking of bread, in the hope that some might be won to Christ by this visual and "dramatic" proclamation of His vicarious death. This "evangelistic" aspect of the Lord's Supper is well expressed in a hymn frequently used by Brethren at their breaking of bread service :

No gospel like this feast
　Spread for Thy church by Thee
Nor prophet nor evangelist
　Preach the glad news so free.
(Elizabeth Rundle Charles)

Once again we believe that this thought of the centrality and simplicity of the Lord's Supper is an important witness to our contemporaries. In an age of organization and sacramentalism such as this, Christians need this constant reminder of the pre-eminent place of Christ and His saving work in the life and witness of the local church.

Furthermore, it is noteworthy that there is nothing more spiritually conducive to fellowship than Christians sharing together in the Lord's Supper. Here is a vital and versatile service that can lend reality to a confession which may otherwise seem nebulous. Paul's question is still relevant, "The bread which we break, is it not a communion of the body of Christ?" (I Cor. 10:16).

It is in fact just their emphasis on the Lord's Supper which, for all their failures, has helped to keep Brethren loyal to Christ and effective, not to mention evangelical. We might also mention briefly that the distinctive Brethren emphasis on the Lord's Supper has given birth to many beautiful hymns which have become part of the treasured heritage of the Christian Church today. Some of these hymns can be found in books such as *Hymns for Christian Worship, Hymns of Light and Love, The Believer's Hymnbook, Hymns and Spiritual Songs, Little Flock Hymnbook*, and *Hymns of Worship and Remembrance*, which are essentially Brethren publications.

Four

Establishing Indigenous Churches

> *"And after some days Paul said unto Barnabas, Let us return now and visit the brethren in every city wherein we proclaimed the word of the Lord, and see how they fare . . . but Paul chose Silas, and went forth, being commended by the brethren to the grace of the Lord. And he went through Syria and Cilicia, confirming the churches"* (Acts 15:36 and 40-41).

AN OUTSTANDING FEATURE OF THE BRETHREN MOVEMENT, particularly the "Open Brethren," has been its evangelistic and missionary effort. Whether in the home-lands or overseas, Brethren are well known for their gospel enterprise. They believe in individual witness by life and lip, and ideally each member regards himself as a missionary-herald of the Saviour. For example, if one of the brethren finds himself transferred to a new locality in the course of his work, he is quite likely to start a Sunday School in his home, or hold cottage meetings for his neighbours. This may continue until there is the nucleus of a local church. If progress is made and it is deemed opportune, a neutral building may then be hired or a chapel erected, and the work will often forge ahead. Should the work grow to large proportions, then consideration will be given to "hiving off" with a view to establishing further assemblies.

Bearing in mind the Matthaean version of the Great Commission : "make disciples . . . baptizing . . . teaching" (Matt. 28:19), as well as the great missionary journeys of Paul, Brethren believe in a policy of church planting and building rather than unrelated evangelism. Through the years they have been marked by pioneer enterprise, and even today it is not unheard of for one or more of their number to go to an unevangelized area with a view to establishing what is sometimes called a "local testimony." Of late, conferences of Brethren have been convened specifically to spark off a more aggressive "expansion," or outreach policy, and to good effect. Indeed, albeit a digression at this point, something must be said about an interesting development among the Brethren in North America.

In some areas of the United States and Canada, independent members of Brethren assemblies have associated to form "pioneer committees." Their idea has been to research and publicize geographical areas of need and then make funds available for suitable building projects and the support of Christian work and workers in new and developing areas.

These "committees" do not seek to dominate or control local churches nor replace their ministry and relieve them of their scriptural responsibilities. They conceive their ministry to be that of handmaids to the assemblies, to make practical help and advice available on the basis of sound research and spiritual maturity. Often they will finance a building programme in an area where a new assembly is getting established. As the assembly develops quite independently of the "committee" or "trust," and achieves stability, it pays off the property loan at a reasonable rate of interest and eventually enjoys ownership of a well-designed and functional building. Alternatively, the committee will assume responsibility as trustees for the building, while the "tenant" assembly meets its financial obligations and maintains its work and witness. There is no attempt at "outside" interference with the day-to-day running of the assembly. As a further development of this programme, Christians in assembly fellowship are encouraged to invest their money in bonds issued by these "committees," so that as well as their receiving regular dividends they know their investment is being used to the furtherance of the Lord's work in which they are interested, at home and overseas. Apart from the many well-appointed chapels that have been erected in recent years, there are now several efficient hospitals (with full-time, commended, staff chaplains), nursing homes, senior citizens' housing complexes and Christian camps, which have either been established or consolidated as a result of this wise, Christian stewardship. Three agencies involved in this ministry are The Stewards Foundation of Chicago (the pioneer in the field), The Calling Foundation of Vancouver, Canada, and The Florida Pioneers. Others are in process of organization.

While this may be regarded as related to physical plant rather than spiritual growth, such efforts have been a great help and encouragement to many assemblies. Through these channels the Brethren have discovered efficient means of development and co-operative effort, without becoming saddled with hierarchical and denominational paraphernalia which, to say the least, is undesirable.

Looking further afield, it is fairly obvious that Brethren have an outstanding record in overseas missionary work. There are about 1,400 "full-time" missionaries working in co-operation with the assemblies in 60 different countries. Beside these, there is a large number of people who, while working in overseas departments of government and business, are involved in Christian missionary work.

Gilbert Kirby, while General Secretary of the Evangelical Alliance, wrote concerning the Christian Brethren in Britain,

In proportion to the size of the Movement there are probably more missionaries drawn from Brethren assemblies, than from any other section of the Protestant

Church in Britain. Brethren missionary work is registered as 'Christian Missions in Many Lands.' There are 625 British Missionaries on the official Prayer List, which makes this the third largest British missionary force. In addition to those working 'on faith lines' in association with the assemblies, others are serving with different interdenominational missions.[1]

Mention must also be made of the great missionary enterprise shown by the North American assemblies, as well as by those of New Zealand. The assemblies of the United States and Canada are represented not only by many missionaries on the field, but also by such great literature movements as the Emmaus Correspondence Courses now running into several millions of copies in 120 different languages (with 11,000 new readers daily), and more recently by Literature Crusades and Mission Corps. It is heartening to observe that there are many assembly young people still willing to dedicate their lives to missionary service.

Brethren missionary work can be traced back to the journeys of Anthony Norris Groves in the 1830's. Such pioneer missionaries as F. S. Arnot (1858–1914), Dan Crawford (1869–1926), F. W. Baedeker (1823–1906), James Lees (1879–1958), and Hudson Taylor (1832–1905) have all been associated with Brethren. Assembly work is particularly strong in Central Africa, India, and South America and they are well represented on almost every mission field of the world today. While we shall not attempt anything like a comprehensive missions survey here, we submit the following facts as worthy of mention.

Today, there are over 400 assembly missionaries in Africa; over 300 in South America, about 360 in Asia and almost 100 in Continental Europe. Work carried on by these missionaries includes among other things :

1. The daily education of some 50,000 children by graduate and trained teachers.

[1] *The Protestant Churches of Britain*, p. 73.

2. The full-time care and treatment of patients, including large numbers of lepers, in over 20 different hospitals (quite apart from local clinics and dispensaries).

3. The production of vast amounts of Christian literature in over 30 different centres. Many of these centres have their own printing presses, in places as far apart as India, Angola, Zambia, Congo, South Africa, Mexico, Venezuela, Ecuador, Honduras and St. Kitts.

4. Broadcasting regularly in over 30 different areas in 28 different languages with at least one regular television programme. Indicative of the millions of listeners being reached is the fact that one assembly radio programme in the Orient has sent out almost one million correspondence courses to date.

5. Caring for young people in children's homes and orphanages.

The most interesting thing about assembly missionary work for our present purpose—and here lies another unique contribution to contemporary Christian witness—is the pattern on which it works. In this as in all else Brethren seek to take the Scriptures as their manual. They have proved to a remarkable degree that modern missions can still be based on New Testament principles.

This means among other things that those who are "commended" to missionary work by the homeland assemblies go forward in direct dependence on God. While the commending assembly or assemblies (sometimes several join in a commendation) by their "commendation" identify themselves with the outgoing missionary, they do not usually guarantee him or her any regular salary. The missionary is regarded as directly responsible to the Lord and therefore "looks to Him" for his support and direction. Having said this, it should be observed that in a responsible, properly-functioning assembly "commendation to the Lord's work" is considered, inter alia, a pledge to prayer, practical interest and concern, and financial support. Fortunately nowadays a much more realistic attitude to "commendation" is being taken than formerly, though there is still considerable room for improvement. (Incidentally, "commendation" is the term generally preferred by Brethren to "commissioning" or "ordination," since they feel it is less sacerdotal or ecclesiastical in its connotation.) It must be said again, in this context, that the method of missionary support traditionally adopted by Brethren is not necessarily the only one possible in the light of Scripture. The Brethren emphasis on the "faith principle" in missionary matters is largely a result of George Müller's very strong emphasis on "living by faith." This man, who became famous for his extraordinary work of caring for orphaned children in the city of Bristol, was not only imbued with a strong missionary interest but also consistently advocated and exemplified the principle of "looking to God alone" for the financial support of Christian work and missionary enterprise. Many spiritually-minded Christians of other "persuasions" have discovered equally honourable ways of supporting the Lord's work and His workers, and it is only proper to recognize this.

When a missionary's effort is crowned with success and local churches are established, these are not regarded as overseas branches of the home church from which the missionary was commended, but independent, indigenous, New Testament churches. These will have their own elders, evangelists and teachers, and the missionary, though sometimes by invitation acting in an advisory capacity, is not in charge or control. Sometimes institutional means such as schools and hospitals prove valuable and, indeed, essential to the establishment of a virile missionary work, but not always.

The Brethren have no missionary society as such, but local assemblies and individual Christians who contribute to the support of missionaries and missionary work use the good offices of such agencies as Echoes of Service of Bath, England; Home and Foreign Mission Funds, Glasgow, Scotland; The Missionary Service Committee of Toronto, Canada; The Fields Inc. of New York, U.S.A.; and The

New Zealand Missionary Funds of Palmerston North, New Zealand. These agencies, if we may so describe them, consider themselves to be the modern counterparts of Epaphroditus of New Testament times. Ideally they do not exercise control or legislate in missionary matters, but exist for the convenience of, and as a channel of contact for, the home assemblies, particularly in such matters as finance and official government representation.

This whole scheme is eminently workable for all its simplicity, and particularly adaptable even in the face of modern nationalistic and totalitarian pressures. It is interesting to notice that the evangelical wing of the Christian church is turning more and more towards this church-centred, New Testament-type mission policy, largely pioneered by Brethren.

Part II

Leadership
in the Churches

"Where no wise guidance is the people falleth, but in the multitude of counsellors there is safety" (Prov. 11:14).

"Tend the flock of God that is your charge, not by constraint but willingly, not for shameful gain but eagerly, not as domineering over those in your charge but being examples to the flock" (I Pet. 5:2, 3, RSV.).

"And then, when the Head Shepherd appears, you will receive for your own the unfading garland of glory" (I Pet. 5:4, NEB.).

Five

Eldership in the New Testament

*"The elders therefore among you I exhort,
who am a fellow-elder, and a witness of
the sufferings of Christ, who am also a
partaker of the glory that shall be revealed:
Tend the flock of God which is among you,
exercising the oversight, not of constraint,
but willingly, according unto God; nor yet
for fithy lucre, but of a ready mind"* (I Pet.
5:1–2).

ONE OF THE GREATEST NEEDS OF OUR LOCAL CHURCHES
today is for strong, spiritual, dedicated and respected
leadership. Perhaps it is the democratic spirit of our age
that has caused us to forget that the local church is a
theocracy, in which the risen Lord rules through chosen
and equipped men. At all events, we shall do well to re-
examine the subject of eldership and ask, "What saith the
Scriptures?"

In this, as in all matters of church polity, it is important
to recognize that the New Testament is not a book of rules,
legal enactments and procedural details. While the Old
Testament prescribes law, rituals and details concerning
the appointment and duties of religious leaders, the New
Testament simply offers general principles. Here in measure
lies the great strength of New Testament ecclesiology, in its

flexibility. Problems and dissent will arise when people try to transform these broad New Testament principles into hard and fast rules. They are intended to be guide lines, not fetters. Their recognition demands spiritual discernment, which is often in shorter supply than lazy attachment to ready-made rules.

If we are to discover God's will concerning the government of local churches we must courageously investigate these New Testament principles. At the same time, we must clearly recognize and if necessary strenuously resist human traditions, no matter how respected their advocates and how effective their application in other historical contexts. History is a good teacher, but it can be a cruel master. If people have abused these important principles and have misapplied them, this in no way invalidates them. Perhaps some of the early Brethren were at fault just here. They were so sick and tired of the sacerdotalism and sectarianism of the official churches of their day that they decided to jettison everything those churches practised, including the recognition of eldership. Darby's doctrine of the "church in ruins" not only despaired of reproducing primitive church order, but rejected eldership as taught and practised in New Testament days.

On the other hand George Müller, a contemporary of Darby's, expresses a more moderate view when writing on the subject of eldership. He states :

1. There should be elders (Matthew 24:45; Luke 12:42; Acts 14:23, 20:17; Titus 1:5; I Peter 5:1).
2. Elders come into office by the appointment of the Holy Ghost (Acts 20:28).
3. Their appointment is made known to them by the secret call of the Spirit (I Timothy 3:1); but is confirmed by the possession of the requisite qualifications (I Timothy 3:2-7; Titus 1:6-9) and by the blessing of God resting upon their labours (I Corinthians 9:2).
4. Saints should acknowledge such and submit to them

in the Lord (I Corinthians 16:15, 16; I Thessalonians 5:12, 13; Hebrews 13:7, 17; I Timothy 5:17).[1]

In reviewing the subject of eldership, we shall first examine relevant scriptures and scriptural terms to try to discover underlying principles. Then we shall examine such matters as the qualifications, responsibilities, appointment and recognition of elders. Finally we shall offer some practical observations.

NEW TESTAMENT TEACHING

There are three areas of the New Testament particularly concerned with the subject of eldership. These are the Acts of the Apostles, the Pastoral Epistles, and the First Epistle of Peter.

(1) *The Acts of the Apostles*

As far as Acts is concerned the subject is first touched on in connection with the Jerusalem church. The elders of the Christian church at Jerusalem were obviously responsible men in whom was vested considerable authority. In fact they shared responsibility in matters of government with the apostles themselves. Their first recorded act was to receive at the hands of Saul and Barnabas the relief sent to Judea by the newly formed church at Antioch (Acts 11:30). Later we see them recognized as co-adjudicators with the apostles concerning questions of doctrine, particularly regarding the terms upon which gentile converts might be accepted into the church (Acts 15:2, 4, 6). Their authority is subsequently underlined by their becoming co-signatories of a letter despatched from the Council of Jerusalem to the gentile Christian churches of Antioch, Syria, and Cilicia. This letter carried by Judas Barsabbas and Silas, "chief men among the brethren," as delegates of the "elder brethren" (v. 23, RV), although not a precedent for later papal encyclicals, at least gives some indication

---

[1] *A Narrative of Some of the Lord's Dealings with George Müller*, Vol. I, p. 276 f.

of the respect in which the elders and their opinions were held in primitive churches (Acts 15:22–3; 16:4; 21:18).

A most significant reference to 'elders' in the Book of Acts is found in chapter 14, "They also appointed elders for them in each congregation, and with prayer and fasting committed them to the Lord in whom they had put their faith" (Acts 14:23). Although this particular passage relates to the churches of Lycaonia (Lystra, Derbe, and Iconium), it was no doubt normal apostolic procedure. The apostles evidently recognized that part of their task of planting indigenous churches was to see that there was due order and respect for properly constituted authority in them.

Another informative passage in Acts on the subject and scope of eldership is found in chapter 20. Here we have the account of Paul's final conversation and counsels to the elders from the church at Ephesus. Paul, in a hurry to reach Jerusalem in time for the Feast of Pentecost, decides to by-pass Ephesus. From Miletus, however, he sends for the Ephesian elders. Having rehearsed his recent experiences, reminded them of his pastoral activities among them, and mentioned his future plans, the Apostle offers the following counsel to them as elders : "Take heed unto yourselves, and to all the flock in which the Holy Ghost hath made you bishops, to feed (literally, 'shepherd') the church of God which he purchased with his own blood" (Acts 20:28). The significance of these words will be discussed later. At least we cannot miss Paul's awareness of the divine authorization of the administrative and pastoral responsibilities of these elders.

(2) *The Pastoral Epistles*

We turn now to Paul's pastoral letters to Timothy and Titus. In these letters, in accordance with common New Testament practice, Paul uses the terms "elder" and "overseer" interchangeably. He talks about such matters as the elder's appointment, dignity, qualifications, and financial support. Special attention should be given to I Timothy 3 and 5, and Titus 1. In I Timothy 4:14, Paul has a significant sentence in which he speaks of the "presbytery", thus viewing the elders corporately.

(3) The First Epistle of Peter

Peter refers to the subject of eldership in the closing chapter of his first epistle. Addressing the elders among his readers, as one who shares their privilege, he speaks of their work as pastors and overseers. He emphasizes the importance of their motives and notes that their great incentive is the return of, and their reward from, the Chief Shepherd (I Pet. 5:1-4).

The only other specific reference to local church "elders" is in James 5:14 where we see them called in to help in a case of sickness. There are, however, two other possible references to elders which are worthy of note. One is in Paul's exhortation to the Romans. There he addresses himself to "he that ruleth" (Rom. 12:8), rendered "a leader" by the NEB. The Apostle may well have the elder in mind, particularly in the light of his use of the same verb (*proistēmi*) in I Tim. 3:4-5 where he is discussing the qualifications of an overseer. The other reference is in I Cor. 12:28 where Paul lists, among the gifts God has set in the Church, "governments." This nautical term *kubernēsis*, normally used to describe a pilot or helmsman, is apparently used here metaphorically to designate those who give leadership in Christian churches, that is the elders.

From these few references, we gather that the elders were important and responsible people in the early Christian churches. Undoubtedly their work then, as now, was sometimes painful, difficult and unrewarding, but thanks to their tireless involvement and spiritual concern the Christians were strengthened, encouraged and preserved from evil doctrines. We can not only observe the wisdom of such divine provision for the government of churches, but also be grateful for it.

Terminology

We must now examine the various New Testament terms used to describe the office and work of elders. First there is the word regularly translated "elder"—*presbyteros*. This word was used unofficially to describe an older person and would be equivalent to our English word "senior" (when used of a person of advanced age), or perhaps more nearly "oldster." Peter uses it thus in I Peter 5:5, immediately after using it "officially" (see NEB). It was also used "officially" in the Septuagint to describe civil and religious leaders. The term was regularly used to describe the Jewish elders of our Lord's day. It combines the two ideas of seniority and dignity.

When the Christian church used this word to describe its leaders, it was doing a perfectly natural thing. As Jews, the first converts to Christianity had grown up with the idea of the elders of the community and congregation. This Jewish office can be traced back to the story of Moses' seventy-man council in Numbers 11. The elders became a permanent features of Jewish life and society. They were responsible councillors and spiritual guides found "in the gate," in the Sanhedrin, and in the synagogue. The term "elder" would be equally meaningful to the Gentile Christians. In Greek society the elders were those who bore responsibility in community life, and handled such matters as taxation, the formulating of laws and the surveillance of morals. It is interesting that this same idea of community leadership is preserved in our word "alderman" (from the Old English "aldor", meaning "patriarch"). In English cities and boroughs an alderman is a councillor next in dignity to the mayor, and a man is not usually elected to this office until he has had considerable experience in local government. Summing up, we may say that in its secular usage *presbyteros* combines the thoughts of maturity and responsibility.

It is unfortunate that etymologically the words "presbyter" and "priest" are associated. The English word "priest" is an abridged form of "prester" which is itself an abbreviation of "presbyter." However, whatever the etymological connection between the words "elder" and "priest," there is never any thought in the New Testament of a Christian elder functioning sacerdotally. In fact while Christians corporately are described as a "priesthood" (I Pet. 2:5 and 9), the New Testament studiously avoids applying the singular "priest" (*hiereus*) to any individual Christian, whether an elder or not. We must disabuse our minds of any sacerdotal thoughts if we would understand the meaning of "elder" in the New Testament.

Another important New Testament word is *episkopos*, regularly translated "overseer" in the RV margin as in the AV text of Acts 20:28. The root of this Greek word is *skopos*, meaning "a watchman." It emphasizes the idea of vigilance, responsibility and care. The translation of *episkopos* by "bishop" is singularly unfortunate, particularly in the light of the later development of the idea of a monarchical episcopate ("bishop" is a derivative of the Old English "biscop", meaning "overseer").

A careful examination of the text shows that the words *presbyteros* (elder) and *episkopos* (overseer) are used interchangeably in the New Testament. For example, Paul sends for the Ephesian *presbyteroi* (elders) and in the course of his address to them calls them *episkopoi* (overseers) (Acts 20:17, 28). He instructs Titus to appoint *presbyteroi* (elders) in every city, but as he proceeds to write of an elder's qualifications he calls him an *episkopos* (overseer). Peter makes a similar identification. He writes : "the *presbyteroi* (elders) therefore among you I exhort . . . exercising the oversight (*episkopountes*), not of constraint, but willingly" (I Pet. 5:1, 2). The fact that these words "elder" and "overseer" are used synonymously in the New Testament is quite significant. Any difference there may be between them is purely in emphasis. "Elder" tends to emphasize maturity, while "overseer" emphasizes responsibility and pastoral function. Jerome writing in the fourth century says, "Among the ancients, bishops and presbyters are the

same, for the one is a term of dignity, the other of age".[1]
The ecclesiastical distinction between the words dates back
to the second century but not earlier.

While dealing with New Testament terminology and
practice, we should note that the presbyter–overseers function corporately. There were several overseers in each local
church. This is borne out in all the passages already quoted
where their appointment and work are referred to. We
may add to these another significant reference, Phil. 1:1.
There Paul addresses himself "to all the saints in Christ
Jesus which are at Philippi, with the bishops (*episkopoi*)
and deacons." Whatever the reasons for the development of
a monarchical episcopate (that is, one "bishop" ruling
several churches) which we find from the second century
onward), this was clearly not New Testament practice. The
evident value of a plurality of overseers will be recognized
immediately if we read the story of Moses' appointment of
other leaders to share responsibility with him in Israel
(Exod. 18:19-27).

As we look at these foregoing scriptures and New Testament terms, certain broad principles become apparent :

i.   Properly constituted New Testament churches recognized divinely appointed and spiritually qualified leadership.

ii. All authority in the local church is derived from Christ
and exercised in His name.

iii. In the New Testament churches government was
collegiate in form rather than monarchical.

iv. Provision was made for the continuation of recognized
rule in the New Testament churches.

v.   There is no special priestly privilege attaching to the
New Testament office of presbyter or overseer. As Lightfoot puts it, "for the most exalted office in the church,
the highest gift of the Spirit, conveyed no sacerdotal
right which was not enjoyed by the humblest member
of the Christian community" (*Philippians*, p. 186).

[1] *Epist.* lxix, cited by J. B. Lightfoot in *Philippians*, p. 98.

So much for scriptural terms and principles related to Church government. We must turn now to the more practical matters of elders' qualifications and service.

QUALIFICATIONS OF AN ELDER

The degree of a man's real influence in a local church depends on his spirituality, and for this reason Scripture lays emphasis on moral and spiritual qualifications for eldership. However, an elder must also have certain natural endowments as well.

Natural Endowments

An elder must be a responsible adult person who is capable of rational thought and intelligent decision. He must be capable of independent and unbiased judgment. He must be a member of the local church where he lives and be known for his integrity and honesty. He must be able to "give and take" in discussion and decision.

If a man suffers from a psychological weakness or instability he is not a suitable candidate for eldership. Similarly, if he is unable to guard confidences, he is unqualified. A certain amount of education and experience in life are practically indispensable for an elder, as well as some understanding of Scripture.

Scriptural Requirements

As we examine the far-reaching qualifications for eldership laid down in Scripture, the two important passages on this subject are I Tim. 3:1-7 and Titus 1:6-9. In each place Paul presents us with a list of virtues and things that should be characteristic of an overseer's life, home, and witness. There are things personal, things domestic, and things social.

(1) Personal Qualifications

The greatest emphasis is placed on personal or "character qualifications" for eldership. God is primarily concerned with a man's moral and spiritual suitability. Analysing these personal qualifications we note the following.

L.C.- C

(a) An elder must be a man of discretion. Paul uses several interesting words to stress this idea of discretion and self-control. He says the elder must be "temperate" (*nēphalios*). This word *nēphalios* literally translated means "not mixed with wine." Used metaphorically as here, it suggests that an elder will not be easily intoxicated by strange emotions and ideas. He will hold things in sober balance. The elder will also be a modest (*kosmios*) man, exercising "self-control" (*enkrateia*) and acting prudently (*sōphronōs*). In other words, he will be a Christian gentleman.

(b) An elder must cultivate a forbearing disposition. He must not be a "brawler" (*paroinos*), literally "quarrelsome because of wine," nor a striker (*plēktēs*). It may seem strange to us that Paul found it necessary to mention such elementary virtues, but we must not forget the low moral standards of his contemporaries. He goes on to say that an elder must be "gentle" (*epieikēs*), that is equitable and fair, always turning his back on the temptation to be contentious" (*amachos*). He must not be "self-willed" (*authadēs*) or "hot-tempered" (*orgilos*). In Paul's day as in ours situations arose which might exasperate those who tried to give leadership among the Christians. These were opportunities to show a Christ-like spirit and must never become "occasions for the flesh."

(c) An elder must show that he has a right sense of values. Here Paul uses two interesting expressions. He says an overseer must not be a "lover of money" (*aphilargyros*), nor "greedy of base gain" (*aischrokerdēs*). Covetousness, then as now, ill became one set to rule in the "house of God." If this warning was needed in New Testament days, how much more so in our acquisitive, materialistic, modern society! Since the love of money is a root of all kinds of evil, it behoves an elder to cultivate a right sense of values. It is easy for a man to become so involved in business responsibilities that he is too busy to function efficiently as an elder.

(d) An elder must give evidence of Christian maturity.

The Apostle expressly forbids the appointment of a new convert (*neophytos*) and states his reason, "for fear the sin of conceit should bring upon him a judgment contrived by the devil" (NEB). Three other words here suggest spiritual maturity. The overseer must be a "lover of good" (*philagathos*), "just" and "holy." Such a person has had time to prove himself an able critic of moral values, and to evidence the sanctity of a life devoted to Christ.

(2) *Domestic Qualifications*

Under this heading we shall note that Paul first emphasizes an elder's conjugal responsibilities, and then his parental obligations.

(a) Conjugal Responsibilities.

The overseer must be the husband of one wife. This, of course, must be understood against the polygamy of Paul's age. He is not denying eldership to an unmarried man, nor to a re-married man, but to a polygamist. There could be no question of moral laxity or unfaithfulness to his marriage vow, if a man was to be considered for eldership.

(b) Parental Obligations.

Concerning parental obligations, the Apostle is even more explicit. A Christian man is responsible for the behaviour and social conduct of his family. He is unqualified for eldership if his children are insubordinate and undisciplined. In his letter to Titus (1:6) the Apostle seems to disqualify from eldership a man whose children have not become Christians. It should be observed here that he probably means that, before the overseer's children reach the age of accountability, and afterwards for that matter, they should give due evidence of respect and control. When they are old enough to decide for themselves in spiritual matters, they should give evidence of a personal commitment to Christ. Obviously, this is a high standard, but we must remember Paul is talking about "elders." If they fail to win their children by godly precept and example and do not exhibit the rudiments of parental discipline in the home, how can they show the spiritual counterparts of those exercises in the church? A man's family and home are a part of his God-given stewardship. As the Apostle puts it, "a man must be of unimpeachable virtue, for he is God's agent in the affairs of His household" (Titus 1:7, JBP).

(3) Social Qualifications

An elder must not only have a good reputation in public but also a genuine desire for the well-being of others.

(a) Public reputation.

It is noteworthy that in both epistles under review an irreproachable character heads the list of elder-qualifications. This man's name must be unsoiled by the slightest suspicion in matters of moral propriety. Whether in the context of the believing community or the unbelieving world, an elder must be "blameless" (*anepilēmptos*, literally, "without reproach") or "unimpeachable" (*anenklētos*). Paul's precise words are, "He must moreover have a good reputation with the non-Christian public, so that he may not be exposed to scandal and get caught in the devil's snare" (I Tim. 3:7, NEB).

The reputation of the local church and that of its leaders are linked. There can be no question of a man's being an overseer if he is the subject of public scandal. Obviously, this does not mean that a man must court a public image, but rather that he should strenuously avoid any public indiscretion or questionable practice. This would probably include "commercial manipulating" and bankruptcy proceedings to say nothing of deliberate, dishonest dealing. Similarly, it proscribes all sexual promiscuity as well as a frivolous attitude to matters of sex, or toward the opposite sex.

(b) Concern for others.

An elder must show a concern for his fellow-Christians. Among these qualifications we read that an overseer-elect should be "given to hospitality." This would be specially meaningful in the early church where the vast majority of the believers were slaves, and consequently often in need of a good meal. For such it would have been a real treat to be welcomed into a Christian home and to sit down to a good meal. An elder would see to it that his home was ever open to the Lord's people. There is still a great need for hospitality today. In this ministry an elder will require the full co-operation of his wife. Indeed, being hospitable, understanding and discreet are among the basic requirements in an elder's wife.

In his concern for others an elder must be "apt to teach." This means that, whether his ministry be in public or in private or both, an overseer must be able to teach others concerning the Christian faith. Sometimes this will mean helping fellow-Christians with problems and showing the "way of God more perfectly". On other occasions it will involve being able to "move his hearers with wholesome teaching and to confute objectors" (Titus 1:9, NEB). He will only be able to do this if, as Paul says, he adheres to the "faithful word." The overseer is committed to the role of defender of the faith. His life and ministry must be a bulwark against the inroads of error.

Six

The Character and Ministry of Elders

"And when they had appointed for them elders in every church, and had prayed with fasting, they commended them to the Lord, on whom they had believed" (Acts 14:23).

An Elder's Appointment

The New Testament lays more emphasis on the task appointed to an elder than on his appointment to the task. However, this is a practical matter and we must give some consideration to it that all things may be done "decently and in order." In this as in other aspects of our subject we must not expect the New Testament to provide rules of procedure, but rather basic, guiding principles. There is room for the use of sanctified common sense and spiritual discernment, under the presidency of the Holy Spirit.

There are three New Testament passages particularly related to the subject; they are Acts 20:28, Acts 14:23 and Titus 1:5. In Acts 20:28, we read, "Take heed unto yourselves and to all the flock in which the Holy Ghost hath made you overseers." Paul here reminds the elders from Ephesus that theirs is a God-given task. They were appointed to their eldership by the Holy Spirit. Since they hold office under God, they must not seek to dominate, but guide. It is important to notice Paul's words, "in which" (*en ho*), mistakenly rendered "over which" in the AV. The use of the preposition *en* emphasizes the idea of service among, rather than supremacy over, the flock. These men are overseers but not overlords.

What Paul does not tell us here is how the Holy Spirit made (*etheto*) these men "overseers," that is, the actual manner of their appointment. True, human appointment is nothing if not by the Holy Spirit, but in this as in other things we are probably not wrong in thinking that "God's methods were men." It may well be that Paul himself, with Timothy, had been involved in the actual, original recognition of the Ephesian elders. The word translated "made" literally means "set," but this gives no clue as to our problem.

Commenting on this point, Professor Bruce says :

Probably the reference to the Holy Spirit here does not mean that their appointment to this sacred ministry had been commanded by prophetic utterance in the church, but rather that they were so appointed and recognized because they were manifestly men on whom the Holy Spirit had bestowed the requisite qualifications for the work.[1]

The second passage reads, "And when they (Paul and Barnabas) had appointed for them (the disciples in the cities of Lycaonia) elders in every church, and had prayed with fasting, they commended them to the Lord, on whom they had believed" (Acts 14:23). The word "appointed" in this verse translates the verb *cheirotoneō*, used only here and in connection with the appointment of the almoner-delegate in II Cor. 8:19. This word, used of voting and meaning literally "to stretch forth the hand," is best taken metaphorically here. In support of this we may note that a compound form of this verb *procheirontoneō* is used to describe a divine appointment in Acts 10:41. Apparently

[1] *New London Commentary—Acts*, p. 416.

the normal New Testament practice was for an apostle or apostolic delegate, as in the case of Titus in Crete (Tit. 1:5), publicly to appoint to eldership those who were spiritually qualified and recognized as such by the church. The verb "ordain" (*kathistēmi*) used in Titus 1:5 confirms this. Commenting on this W. E. Vine says:

> The Revised Version translates it (*kathistēmi*) by 'appoint' in Titus 1:5, instead of 'ordain,' of the elders whom Titus was to appoint in every city in Crete. Not a formal ecclesiastical ordination is in view, but the appointment for the recognition of the churches, of those who had already been raised up and qualified by the Holy Spirit, and had given evidence of this in their life and service.[1]

With these passages in mind, we must ask ourselves how this practical appointment of overseers is to be carried out in our day. Professor Blaiklock's comment on Acts 14:23 is perhaps apropos here. He writes,

> The basic arrangement seems to have been the appointment of elders, an eminently sensible scheme, in tune with common secular practice, which in no way interfered with the emergence of gifted leadership of other types, for example, the "prophets and teachers."[2]

The following ideals must be borne in mind. There must be no appointment of those whom the Holy Spirit has not signified as fitted by Him. While there is no exact statement in the New Testament which says that eldership is a charismatic ministry, unless it be Romans 12:8 "he that ruleth with diligence" or I Corinthians 12:8, this is plainly the inference. Since the government of a local church is an important part of an overseer's work, it follows that he will be concerned with his fellow-elders in the perpetuation of orderly rule in it. In normal practice, therefore, it would appear that the elders, acting corporately and conscious of the sovereign Spirit's direction, appoint other elders.

[1] *Expository Dictionary of New Testament Words*, Vol. I, p. 67.
[2] *Tyndale New Testament Commentary—Acts*, p. 109.

Some practical pointers about the preparation of younger men for responsibility in the local church will be given later.

Some other practical problems in relation to overseer appointment must be touched on here. What happens in the case of a newly-formed, local church? Who is responsible for the appointment of its elders? Circumstances vary, but in general there are two ways in which a local church comes into being. Either a parent church decides to "hive off" or a pioneer missionary or worker gathers a group of converts together. In the former case, if the "parent church" shows good judgment, it will make available some of its elders for the overseeing of the "daughter church." This does not mean limiting the autonomy of the new assembly. In the context of this newly constituted assembly, these elders will act independently, under God. If, from time to time, they wish to consult with the brethren in the "parent" assembly, then obviously this is their prerogative. They will, of course, be wise to remember that the new assembly is not a branch church but a completely autonomous one.

In the case of a local church planted through the ministry of a "missionary," he will, as a matter of course, instruct his converts in matters of church policy, and urge certain fitted individuals to assume responsibility. There would probably be consultation with other respected servants of the Lord. Then at a formal meeting of the church those marked as overseers might be duly presented and publicly recognized.

One other situation calls for a comment: that of an established church which for one of a number of different reasons has never had proper care or government. Suppose it is exercised about eldership, but because of the problem of personalities and such like it hardly knows how to begin. There are several possible courses open to such an assembly. Perhaps the procedure in the case of the recently-pioneered church might be adopted. Usually there are respected and beloved servants of Christ well known to the local church.

After a period of prayer, visitation, and ministry, the Lord's servant could be asked to point out gifted men who might exercise responsibility. These men might then be set forward, and appointed after due prayer and opportunity having been given to the church to express itself.

Of course, there is no need to involve any outside party. Usually there are one or two men who enjoy the confidence of the entire church. Let these men, as exercised before the Lord, associate others with themselves and then on a suitable occasion, after due consideration, come before the cnurch for formal recognition. There are always exceptional and difficult cases, but usually things can be resolved amicably and for God's glory, if undertaken in love and out of complete deference to the sovereign Lord in His Church.

AN ELDER'S MOTIVES

The value of an elder's work lies not so much in what he does as in why he does it; hence the need for examining motives. Peter emphasised this in his exhortations to the "fellow-elders" (*synpresbyteroi*) (I Pet. 5:1-4). He notes three things in this regard :

(1) An elder must fulfil his ministry "willingly, according unto God, and not of constraint." This suggests that a man must discover the mean between unhealthy reluctance and overweening ambition if he is to be effective as an elder. Some men are extremely ambitious for office and power, and because of this the unfortunate circumstance sometimes arises in a local church that the least qualified and least spiritual dominate. Those whom God has called and fitted for this task must not, through false modesty or a retiring disposition, decline the responsibility of leadership. Ultimately, of course, all Christian service must be done not out of the constraint of a sense of duty, but because of the "constraining love of Christ." This was made abundantly plain by Christ who, before commissioning Peter to his pastoral responsibilities, asked

for the confession of his love. The Apostle never forgot
this divine order. An elder can never have too much of
the love of Christ in his heart (see John 21:15-17).

(2) An elder must serve with a view to giving rather
than getting. Peter adds, "nor yet for filthy lucre, but of
a ready mind." An elder should be characterized by an
alacrity to serve rather than to be served. This does not
deny the scriptural principle of financial reward for a
man who spends his time in serving the Lord and His
people. Rather does it point out the danger of harbouring such unworthy motives as desire for pecuniary gain.

(3) An elder must cultivate a humble spirit in the discharging of his God-given stewardship. There can be no
place for pride in the elder. His task has been given him
by God and he must not display a domineering attitude
in his discharging of it. Peter says, "neither as lording it
over the charge (*klēros*) allotted to you." The word
klēros involves the idea of apportionment by lot. It is
God who grants a man the stewardship of being a leader.
An elder must realize that it is not his to have the "final
say" but God's. If he forgets this, he will quickly become
another Diotrephes, not only cultivating his own narrow
interests but also hurting other people's feelings.

TEACHING AND SHEPHERDING

The New Testament makes it abundantly plain that eldership is no sinecure. Generally speaking there are two main
areas of responsibility for an elder. On the one hand he
must be able to teach and give pastoral help and counsel to
the Christians; on the other he must be able to oversee and
guide in the spiritual life and affairs of the church as a
whole.

The elder's most important lesson is that of his own life.
For this reason Peter writes, "making yourselves ensamples
to the flock". The word *typos* conveys the idea of a model
or pattern. Peter is suggesting that the elder must ever
bear in mind that people will be patterning their lives on
his. As a spiritual guide, he is responsible to see that his

life is worth copying. Paul has the same thing in mind when he says to the Ephesian elders, "Keep watch over yourselves and over all the flock . . ." (Acts 20:28 NEB). He is not telling them to look out for their own interests first, but rather to be vigilant about their own conduct. The author of Hebrews puts it another way. He says, "Remember your leaders, those who first spoke God's message to you; and reflecting upon the outcome of their life and work, follow the example of their faith" (Heb. 13:7, NEB). The phrase "follow the example of their faith" reads literally "imitate their faith" (*mimeisthe tēn pistin*).

We have already noted that the overseer must be "apt to teach." This undoubtedly envisages an oral, teaching ministry, but it includes much more. An elder will teach privately, and on the basis of his "holding to the faithful word" (Titus 1:9), will be ready to answer questions and clarify the beliefs of others. Many a godly overseer has taught invaluable lessons concerning belief and behaviour without mounting the pulpit steps.

The pastoral ministry devolving on an elder has often received scant notice. Scripture leaves us in no doubt as to this important area of responsibility. Paul says, "Shepherd (*poimanein*) the church, that is, tend and feed and guide the church of the Lord . . ." (Acts 20:28, Amp.). In Heb. 13:17 Christian leaders are described as "tireless in their concern for you, as men who must render an account" (NEB). Peter writes, "tend that flock of God whose shepherds you are" (I Pet. 5:2 NEB); and goes on to mention the appearing of the "Chief Shepherd," thus by implication viewing his fellow elders as under-shepherds.

In what, we may ask, does this ministry of shepherding consist? In order to answer this question let us look at the "Shepherd Psalm" and observe the ministry of Jehovah, the Shepherd. The basic idea of Psalm 23 is that of the Shepherd's personal provision for the sheep. He provides pasture, guidance, companionship, comfort, protection, discipline, and a home. The spiritual counterparts of these in relation to the ministry of eldership are obvious but worthy of further comment and practical application.

(1) *Spiritual Food.* While it is true that the elder, as an under-shepherd, must provide nourishing spiritual food, it does not necessarily follow that he will always personally administer it. From the practical view of the day to day life of the local church it certainly does point out the need for elders to provide a balanced diet. This may mean planning a syllabus of subjects or using the services of those who have been gifted to the church by the risen Christ as evangelists or "pastor-teachers." It will mean careful consideration being given to the food with which the saints are fed. There is need for consecutive, expository preaching of the Word of God.

(2) *Guidance.* Similarly, there is great need for the ministry of guidance. This will include all kinds of spiritual counselling. There will be people with personal, domestic, and marital problems. The elder who makes himself available for such a counselling ministry will come face to face with the confusion of modern living. Sometimes he will be bewildered, even shocked beyond words. He will be cast on God in prayer and, conscious of his own utter dependence and frailty, will seek to guide erring and lost sheep into the warmth of the flock and the fellowship of the Chief Shepherd. Only as the elders are walking "in the paths of righteousness" will the sheep follow in them.

(3) *Companionship.* One of the afflictions of our contemporary society is loneliness. The pace and involvement of modern living leave few people with time, and fewer still with care, for their fellows. Even within the church there are many who feel left out and unwanted. They lack an outgoing disposition and do not make friends easily. Perhaps through circumstances beyond their control they have been uprooted and transferred to an almost alien society. Older people watch their friends depart one by one. Often their life's partner has pre-deceased them and they have begun to feel unwanted and alone. These are opportunities for under-shepherds. Lonely sheep can be

drawn in by love, concern and consideration. It is the responsibility of all, but especially of the overseer, to keep an open eye for the lonely who need companionship.

(4) *Comfort.* There come to all "the shadows of the valley." It is in them that we come into a "second-person-experience" of the Good Shepherd. It is no longer "He" who guides, but "Thou who art with me." However, this is often made real and experimental through the good offices of an under-shepherd. To whom, humanly speaking, can a bereaved believer turn in the great hour of need? The undertaker may be skilled in his ministration; the family, if near, can be a great help, but how urgently needed are the solicitudes of the godly elder. Visitation may be time-consuming, even tedious, but home-going elders make for church-going people.

(5) *Protection.* The young, the sick and the spiritually weak need protection. There are wolves set to devour and destroy the flock and the under-shepherd's staff of protecting love is greatly needed. Sometimes it will take the patience of a Job and the understanding of a Solomon, but the greatest need is for the love of Christ.

(6) *Discipline.* Then there is the responsibility of discipline. Sinning saints, like wandering sheep, must sometimes smart under the rod of correction. Correction is always the task of the spiritual, and is administered in a spirit of humility (Gal. 6:1). No one is beyond temptation and the elder must always act in "self-consideration" as well as Christlike love. However, there is no grace in compromise. Discipline, for whatever reason, should always be done with a view to restoration. The idea is to heal, not hurt, although sometimes there must be hurt to heal. There are few more delicate tasks than those falling to the lot of under-shepherds.

(7) *A Home.* When we think of a home we think of warmth, family love, and loyal friends. This too is a part of the elder's ministry, to make sure that the assembly is a spiritual home for the people of God. In New Testament days the churches met in homes, and this was not without

advantage. Even in our age of buildings and fine facilities the spirit of a home can still be cultivated. If an elder recognizes in the church an undue emphasis on age distinction or social advantage or intellectual attainment, he must do all within his power, in fellowship with his fellow elders, to cultivate the "unity of the Spirit in the bond of peace."

Paul's exhortation to the Thessalonians contains some helpful suggestions about the onerous responsibilities of elders (I. Thess. 5:12-14). While the main emphasis of this passage, as we shall observe later, is on the need for the proper recognition of leaders or elders, it throws valuable light on their work. In general, their task is three-fold. They work hard among the Christians in the local church; they bear the burden of authority and leadership under Christ; and they offer admonition when required (v. 12). The Apostle becomes even more specific in verse 14 (which is best referred to these elders). He reminds them that they have these responsibilities, among others : (i) to admonish the disorderly, (ii) to encourage the fainthearted, (iii) to support the weak, and (iv) to be longsuffering to all.

Obviously a faithful elder will not be wandering around looking for work !

ADMINISTRATIVE RESPONSIBILITIES

Turning now to the governmental responsibilities of overseers, we see that Peter and Paul place considerable emphasis here. Peter exhorts his fellow-elders to "exercise the oversight" in the flock. Paul reminds the elders at Miletus that they are "overseers." Writing to the Thessalonian church, the apostle speaks of their leaders as "over them in the Lord" (I Thess. 5:12). (His use of the word *proistēmi* here suggests rule or presidency as in Rom. 12:8 and I Tim. 3:4-5.) The elders are Christ's vicegerents in the church, and as such are to be obeyed and respected. Of course, they must earn the respect of their fellow-Christians by a godly walk and wise administration.

One of the evidences of divine wisdom in the patterning of the local church is seen in the collegiate form of government. By regular and confidential discussion, as directed by the Holy Spirit through the Scriptures, elders will together come to decisions that effect the development and activity of the church. No one individual will have to bear the load of responsibility, but the elders will share the burden. All the details of administrative and pastoral work can be undertaken collectively, and in this as in most things "two heads are better than one." It should be pointed out here that, whereas deacons will concern themselves with the material, financial, and physical needs of the church, elders will be concerned with its spiritual well-being.

There are several New Testament examples of this corporate activity of elders. In the Jerusalem church we see them presiding over administrative affairs (Acts 11:30; 15:2, 4, 6; 16:4). At Lystra we see the elders lay hands on Timothy as, in obedience to a prophetic oracle, they commission him to Christian service (cf. I Tim. 4:14 with Acts 16:1-3). We have an almost identical incident taking place at Syrian Antioch, when Barnabas and Saul are commended to the Lord's work (Acts 13:1-3). In the short, early Epistle of James with its obvious background of synagogue procedure, we see the leaders summoned to a sick bed, praying together and anointing a Christian for healing.

While dealing with this subject of corporate administration, some practical observations must be made regarding the "elders' council" or, as it is sometimes called, "the oversight meeting." Such sessions to be effective will be held on a regular basis and convened in orderly fashion. Due thought and prayer will be given to matters in hand and decisions will be made and implemented. If an agenda is circulated in advance with a view to private consideration and prayer, this will greatly facilitate discussion and save time. A chairman, official minutes and an orderly procedure would seem to be in accord with the well-known words of Scripture, "But let all things be done decently and in order" (I Cor. 14:40). Absolutely nothing is to be gained from the unorganized approach which is mistakenly supposed to allow freedom to the Spirit. His work is always orderly, and He will be both honoured and more likely to reveal His will in an ordered setting. This does not rule out extra-circular discussion, or a complete freedom of expression on all subjects, always in love.

These practical matters may helpfully be born in mind with regard to an "oversight meeting":

(1) Overseers should beware of becoming involved in lengthy discussions about peripheral details. Those things which might be regarded as "deacon-matters" are best handled by small working committees.

(2) Time is essential, but meetings should start and end on time. Oversight meetings (sometimes called "over-night meetings") are notorious for their prolixity.

(3) The service of a good chairman is invaluable, especially if he has the ability to keep discussion "to the point," and keep the meeting moving.

(4) After a meeting has been called to order and begun in an atmosphere of prayer, a roll call is good if only for its psychological effect. Absentees will recognize the courtesy of an explanation of their absence. After all, an elder's work is serious and responsible business, and should be treated as such.

(5) A reading and approval of the minutes is most helpful for exactness, understanding and reference.

(6) It is usually wise not to make a decision on an important issue the first time it appears on the agenda. The principle of "waiting on the Lord" is a sound one. Of course emergencies call for emergency treatment, but these are rare.

(7) It is much easier for elders to make particular decisions if general principles of procedure have been agreed upon and accepted. Particular cases may involve new problems, but it is wise to recognize, and to beware of establishing, precedents without due thought.

(8) Decisions should be made carefully without fear or favour, and always in love.

(9) Once a decision has been made by the oversight, no

individual elder should go against it whether it be to his personal liking or not. Furthermore, no segment of the oversight should make decisions apart from the knowledge of the whole group.

(10) Minor executive functions may wisely be allocated to responsible individuals to obviate the necessity of calling a full elders' meeting to decide details.

(11) When a task is allocated to an individual elder or small committee, progress reports should be expected and given.

(12) Candour, "sweet-reasonableness" (Phil. 4:5), commonsense, a knowledge of the Scriptures, concern for people, and a love for Christ will help in any elders' meeting.

It goes without saying that if a man cannot control his tongue or temper, he is disqualified from attending such meetings, and probably from being an overseer. Tolerance there will be, honesty there must be, as well as privacy. Confidential discussions in the council chamber are definitely not for retailing in public.

There will necessarily be a spirit of "give and take." An individual should not demand recognition of his programme if it is clearly not the will of the majority. Majority decisions are not always right in secular discussions, but as the Bible says, "in the multitude of counsellors there is safety" (Prov. 11:14). If spiritual elders have prepared by prayer before attending the "oversight meeting," there is little likelihood of final dissent. Where there is difference of opinion, this can often be resolved after prayer together and examination of Scripture. In important matters of principle, unanimity would seem desirable but in most procedural matters the majority should rule. The demand for unanimity can sometimes be a manoeuvre of dissident factions and a very thin camouflage for minority rule.

Before leaving this subject of the elders' corporate rule and pastoral responsibility, something must be said about making sure the whole assembly is being "tended." In a large assembly it might be helpful if certain areas of responsibility are delegated to individual elders. This will save time and repetitious action. It does not mean that the others will neglect these "allocated areas," nor will it mean the delegated elder is solely responsible. He is answerable to the elders as a body under God. In a well-governed assembly, every particular facet of the work will come up for regular review with a view to getting things done.

This also applies in the matter of pastoral contact. It is much more practical for each elder to have so many families under his personal surveillance. This will mean a check on absentees, and an over-all pastoral effectiveness. Scriptural precedent may be found for this in Exodus 12:21 which suggests that the elders in Israel bore responsibility for certain families. In this too there must be constant vigil and regular checking and reporting back to the oversight. None of these things will guarantee success but all else being equal they will facilitate the shouldering of responsibility. The conscientious overseer today, like his counterpart in New Testament days, will still experience sleepless nights (see Heb. 13:17, NEB).

Seven

The Recognition and Training of Elders

*". . . esteem them exceeding highly in love
for their work's sake"* (I Thess. 5:13).

Recognition of Elders

IT IS SOMETIMES ARGUED THAT SINCE ELDERSHIP IS A
ministry rather than an office there need be no formal
recognition of individuals as elders. While it is true that
the exercise of eldership is the important thing, it cannot
be denied that in New Testament days elders were known
and identified as leaders in this or that local church. Their
office was nothing apart from their work, but they were
divinely authorized and locally recognized. The Scriptures
already referred to (e.g. Acts 11:30; 15:2; 16:4; 21:18)
indicate that in the Jerusalem church there was a recognized group of men called "the elders," who associated
with the apostles for purposes of rule. Further, when Paul
sent to Ephesus from Miletus and called for the elders of
the church, they were a well-known body and they
responded without hesitation (Acts 20:17, 28). In addressing his epistle to the church at Philippi, Paul writes "to
all the saints in Christ Jesus which are at Philippi, with
the 'overseers' and deacons." This suggests a definite group
of people who, while members of the Philippian church,
were distinguishable within it as leaders.

Other important words in this connexion are found in Paul's First Epistle to the Thessalonians noted earlier, "We beg you, brothers, to acknowledge those who are working so hard among you, and in the Lord's fellowship are your leaders and counsellors. Hold them in the highest possible esteem and affection for the work they do" (I Thess. 5:13, NEB). Commenting on these words, Dr. Leon Morris writes, "This means that the people in question are elders, for they alone would exercise the triple function." Rejecting the idea of informal leadership. Dr. Morris continues,

> But elders were appointed from the earliest times (Acts 11:30; 14:23, etc.), and, from the model of the Jewish synagogue, elders are to be expected even in very young churches. It may be possible for an organization to exist without officebearers of any kind; but it is far from usual, and such evidence as we have does not indicate that the early church made the attempt.[1]

The writer of the Epistle to the Hebrews has a similar passage: "Remember your leaders and superiors in authority . . . obey your spiritual leaders and submit to them—continually recognizing their authority over you; for they are constantly keeping watch over your souls and guarding your spiritual welfare, as men who will have to render an account [of their trust]" (Heb. 13:7, 17, Amp). Two other passages will suffice to demonstrate the primitive churches' recognition of their elders as distinct governing bodies. Paul reminds Timothy of the occasion when the elders as a body "laid hands on him", and writes, "Do not neglect the spiritual endowment you possess, which was given you, under the guidance of prophecy, through the laying on of the hands of the elders as a body" (I Tim. 4:14, NEB). Then Peter's words to his fellow-elders seem to indicate the same thing. He writes: "The elders, therefore, among you. . . ." (I Pet. 5:1).

In fact, it is noteworthy that in New Testament days

---

[1] *Thessalonians*, Tyndale N.T. Commentary, p. 98.

elders were not only definitely recognized but shown the utmost respect. No doubt this too would be a carry-over from Judaism, where the "elders" were accorded respect little short of reverence. Further, we observe that individual elders as well as the "presbytery," were to be honoured, and never lightly slandered. Paul writes, "Against an elder receive not an accusation, except at the mouth of two or three witnesses" (I Tim. 5:19). This may refer to the respect due an older person, but in its context it is probably a reference to an overseer.

It is unfortunate, to say the least, that the contemporary lack of respect for established authority has rubbed off on the church. The practical recognition of the headship of Christ in the assembly may well be expressed in our respect and love for those whom He has equipped to be its guides.

The Support of Elders

In their desire to escape the shackles of officialdom in ecclesiastical matters, Brethren have usually gone to the other extreme of neglecting the practical recognition and support of a "whole time" ministry within the context of a local church. Writing to Timothy on this subject Paul says, "Elders who do well as leaders should be reckoned worthy of a double stipend (*timēs*), in particular those who labour at preaching and teaching. For Scripture says 'a threshing ox shall not be muzzled'; and besides, 'the workman earns his pay'" (I Tim. 5:17, NEB). The word *timēs*, translated "stipend" by the NEB, might be rendered "honorarium."[1] From the context and supporting quotations, which incidentally are from the Old Testament (Deut. 25:4) and New Testament (Luke 10:7) respectively and are described together as "Scripture," the meaning of Paul's language is plain. Elders who give their time to ministry in a local church should be financially supported by that church. It would be particularly beneficial in our

---

[1] See Vine: *Expository Dictionary of New Testament Words*, Vol. II, p. 230.

age of involvement in other things, including the legitimate pursuit of making a living, if assemblies would give more practical expression to this eminently wise arrangement.[1] As Professor Bruce puts it : "Those who devote part or the whole of their time to the spiritual care of the church have a right to have their material needs supplied by the church, in part or in whole."[2]

Such an arrangement would call for considerable sacrifice on the part of the man, or men, who are engaged in this local pastoral and teaching ministry, but there will be rich spiritual dividends for all. The recognition and support of this kind of ministry does not mean a so-called "one-man ministry," nor does it in any way militate against the doctrine of "the priesthood of all believers."

TENURE OF OFFICE

Another practical matter calling for consideration is the elder's tenure of office. Does it follow "once an elder, always an elder"? Is there such a thing as retirement from eldership? Can an elder be dismissed for any reason? Before seeking to answer such questions, we must remind ourselves again that the New Testament is not a book of rules and regulations. There must always be a place for the exercise of informed, spiritual judgement.

Regarding the perpetuity of an elder's ministry we shall do well to recognize that the New Testament emphasis is on the exercise of oversight rather than on terms of office. Therefore, if a man is capable of fulfilling his ministry as an elder, he should continue to be recognized in the

[1] Guthrie, who regards *timēs* as referring to remuneration of "officials of the Church," writes : "Whatever the Apostle is here citing, he intends Timothy to understand that a divine sanction underlies the principle of fair provision for those who serve the Church. Too often a niggardly attitude has been maintained towards faithful men who have laboured for Christ in the interest of others. The Apostle has already deplored money-grabbing (iii.3.) but he equally deplores inadequate remuneration." *The Pastoral Epistles*, Tyndale N.T. Commentary, p. 106.

[2] *New Testament Church in 1955*, p. 45.

assembly. It does not follow that when an elder leaves one assembly because of a change of residence he will automatically be received as an elder in another assembly. In this latter case other considerations will need to be borne in mind, such as winning the brethren's confidence, though naturally, since his commendation will refer to the transferring elder's integrity and service, the receiving assembly will give special thought to his case. Experience, spiritual maturity, and the qualities of an elder are always in short supply.

The question of retiring from eldership raises all kinds of issues. Each case must be judged on its own merit and in the light of Scripture and Christian charity. Age is not the criterion; indeed, many an older man, retiring from business, has become a much more effective elder. The emphasis is on maturity not seniority. If a man has become senile and therefore incapable of decision and active participation in church matters, it would be a wise and gracious gesture for him to withdraw from the elders' council. His advice might still be valuable on occasion. In any case, great care must be taken not to hurt such a man or to make him feel unwanted. Sometimes it might be wise if elders who are advanced in years were given a more consultative capacity. There is danger in clinging to an office beyond the time of one's effectiveness. H. St. John offers the following wise words on this subject :

> Surely, a godly man who knows that his ministry, and his powers of expression, are definitely waning, will submit to discipline, and be prepared to retire into the shadows. But I do not think it would be right to take an elder brother, who may have served a particular church, off the oversight. I would sooner allow him to act as a sort of emeritus professor, giving him still the opportunity of doing what he can, while at the same time he will learn to grow old gracefully.[1]

The story of the Levites may be helpful here. Compar-

[1] *New Testament Church in 1955*, p. 52.

ing the words of Numbers 4:3, 23, 30 with 8:24, it appears that from the age of 25 to 30 years a Levite was under apprenticeship. Then, after his novitiate, he gave 20 years of active service. At the age of 50 he withdrew from active service and assumed an advisory role (Num. 8:25-26).

Dismissal of an elder would be a delicate situation calling for the utmost care and tact. Presumably such a thing would happen only if a man has proved himself unworthy of eldership through sin, heresy or impossible obstinacy. There are as noted scriptural qualifications for eldership and a man must be honest before God in the light of these. To strike a practical note here, while the whole church as such does not appoint its elders, it is not a bad idea for all the members to be given regular opportunity to write down the names of those whom they themselves recognize as elders. This information can then be considered prayerfully and confidentially by the elders and may give rise to exercise of heart before the Lord. We cannot expect perfection but there should be evidence of an elder's humbly aiming at divinely-appointed goals.

THE TRAINING OF ELDERS

Scripture is full of examples of leaders who trained others to assume responsibility after them. Paul envisages this. Writing to Timothy he says, "And the things which thou hast heard from me among many witnesses, the same commit thou to faithful men, who shall be able to teach others also" (II Tim. 2:2). No doubt he had more than training for eldership in mind, but Paul certainly would have included this.

A man will not become an elder overnight, and the better his training the more effectively will he fulfil his ministry. Older men of experience will take definite steps to prepare young men in matters of oversight. These younger men will be taught by association, example and precept to assume responsibility and leadership. They will "sit in" on elders' discussions, accompany elders on visitation, and if they have a gift for oral ministry will be given opportunity to exercise it. Such prayerful preparation will be good for the older as well as the young men; and the blending of experience and enthusiasm will be to mutual profit. It will call for consideration on both sides, and will teach men the important lessons of co-operation and tolerance.

When these younger men have shown capability and maturity and the overseers feel the time for their recognition has come, definite steps should then be taken to inform the church. It would be wise if there be opportunity for expressions of confidence from the church as a whole. There is no reason why there should not be a service of thanksgiving and dedication. The elders might then publicly lay hands on those who are joining them in shouldering the privilege and responsibility of tending the flock. This would identify them as "fellow-workers in God's service."

Pitfalls to be Avoided

It will help us if we recognize some of our mistakes and then, as helped of God, seek to correct them and avoid similar ones.

(1) We must admit that very often among those known as "Brethren" things have been done too haphazardly. In this matter of eldership we have often taken the easy line of accepting popular nomination rather than the Holy Spirit's direction. Men have been regarded as qualified because of their prominence in society, their financial achievements, or their business acumen. Undoubtedly natural abilities are important, and experience in society can help a man, but these are not valid criteria for eldership. Often the man who is recognized as equipped to serve as an elder will be successful in secular and social matters, but not necessarily so. There must be complete honesty and due recognition of spiritual values if the oversight is to be respected and effective.

(2) On occasion undue prominence has been given to individuals whose doubtful claim to recognition has been

their ability to talk, and never listen to the opinions of others. Assemblies have sometimes been ruined by the imposing on them of the traditional interpretations of very determined so-called "elders" who, though not lacking in doctrine, have been utterly lacking in grace.

(3) There has sometimes been an undue emphasis on the democratic principle of government. This has led to a breakdown of discipline, a complete lack of rule and little real evidence of spiritual leadership. We have run so far from the idea of one-man rule that we have settled for an everyman rule.

(4) There has been a sad neglect of the pastoral side of eldership and men whose commission is to "tend the flock" have become immersed in the minutiae of material matters. Although the lines are not clearly laid down in the New Testament, there seems to be a distinction between deacon-work and "overseeing."

(5) Many local churches have suffered from a lack of communication between the overseers and the congregation at large. There can be no doubt that while the elders are finally responsible in government, they have a duty to keep the church informed in matters of policy and practice. The believers can pray intelligently, and offer help, only if they are kept informed. This does not mean the divulging of confidential information, but rather keeping the lines of communication open. The church will then have confidence in its elders and will know that they are responsible and interested men who have a care for the assembly.

(6) All too little consideration has been given to the orderly exposition of the Scripture and scriptural truth. Too much has been left to the discretion and personal preference of visiting speakers. More thought should be given by elders to the provision of suitable and competent ministry under the guidance of the Holy Spirit.

(7) There is an evident lack of purposeful planning. Often we have failed to examine our goals and decide on long-term plans. We have adopted Micawber's philosophy and are sitting waiting for something good to turn up.

Certainly we must live in the light of the Advent of Christ but we must become more purposeful in our planning which, in any case, will always be subject to His will.

(8) There has been all too little inter-church co-operation and understanding. Often elders have been too parochial in their thinking with the result that barriers and personality feuds have grown to ridiculous proportions. While recognizing the autonomy of each local church, we must cultivate the fellowship of all the people of God. There is a great need today for a visible expression of the catholicity of the Church.

A Noble Task

In conclusion we must say something about the elder's great incentive and reward. Writing of these Peter says, "And when the chief Shepherd shall be manifested, ye shall receive the crown of glory that fadeth not away" (I Pet. 5:4). The Apostle knew how difficult the task of tending the flock could be. There were weak and sick lambs, habitual wanderers, sheep who were always butting and fighting, as well as obstinate rams. The under-shepherd will soon become discouraged if he forgets the appearing of the Chief Shepherd, whose heart throbs with love for every member of the flock.

Let the elder ever remember that long after the kicks and rebuttals, the misunderstanding of friends and foe alike, and the sleepless nights have faded into oblivion, the amaranthine crown received from the nail-pierced hand of Christ will remain fresh. He will enjoy the unspeakable privilege of sitting in glory with Him who, as the Good Shepherd, died to save the sheep, as the Great Shepherd rose to preserve them, and as the Chief Shepherd comes to escort them, that they may "dwell in the house of the Lord forever."

"If any man aspires to eldership he is setting his heart on a noble task" (I Tim. 3:1, lit.).

Part III

Ministry and Service in the Churches

*"The prophet that hath a dream, let him tell a dream;
and he that hath my word, let him speak my word
faithfully.
What is the straw to the wheat? saith the Lord.
Is not my word like as fire? saith the Lord;
and like a hammer that breaketh the rock in pieces?"*
(Jer. 23:28, 29).

Eight

Declaring the Whole Counsel of God

> "Whom will he teach knowledge? And whom will he make to understand the message? Them that are weaned from the milk, and drawn from the breasts? For it is precept upon precept, precept upon precept; line upon line, line upon line; here a little, there a little" (Isa. 28:9-10).

OBVIOUSLY ONE VITAL INGREDIENT IN THE LIFE OF A local church is the ministry of the Word of God. Without the faithful and clear exposition of the Word that gave the churches their birth they are unlikely to survive, let alone multiply. The ancient commandment "He that hath My Word let him speak it!" is still to be obeyed. Those who fail to obey must still answer the question accompanying that command, "What is the straw to the wheat?"

Now there are many ways in which this task can be tackled and Brethren have been foremost in demonstrating the feasibility of what might be called in other circles a "lay ministry." They have in the past encouraged young men to study their Bibles with a view, among other things, to sharing their discoveries with others by way of oral ministry or preaching. This has been very beneficial and many a man who might have occupied the "silent

pew" in another type of ecclesiastical setting has been an
active preacher in Brethren circles. This is good, and
providing there is due recognition of the scriptural principle
that spiritual endowment alone qualifies for ministry, it will
be fruitful.

However, there must be due care and thought in this
whole area lest we become too haphazard and negligent of
our responsibility to offer an orderly and relevant ministry
of the Word. It is all too easy for us to allow the pendulum
to swing to extremes. In refusing the evident extremes of
officialdom and professionalism in certain ecclesiastical
circles, we must guard against the other extreme of refusing
the exercise of a pastoral, teaching ministry. Properly
exercised, such ministry will stimulate rather than stifle
other gifts in the local church. In this section we shall
examine some of the possibilities in the area of the preaching of God's Word.

In the Early Church there were evidently gifted elders
who, while not exercising a spoken ministry, were recognized for their administrative and spiritual ability. They
were known as "elders that rule", and were to be accorded
due respect (I Tim. 5:17; Rom. 12:8; I Thess. 5:12). However, whether an elder was a speaker or an administrator
he bore the responsibility of "feeding the flock of God"
(I Pet. 5:2) and that included making adequate provision
for the spiritual diet of the people of God.

This leads us to a consideration of a very important and
practical subject, all too easily overlooked in contemporary
assembly gatherings : the provision and maintenance of an
adequate ministry of the Word of God.

Purposeful Planning

If the preaching and teaching ministries of an assembly
are to be effective, it is vital that they be the expression of
a definite and considered purpose. Scripture teaches that
all things are to be "done decently and in order" (I Cor.
14:40), and this applies to oral ministry. Strange to relate,
there are still individuals who imagine that there is some-

thing more spiritual about the haphazard and disorganized than the arranged.

Now in the context of our discussion, it may be asserted that it is the elders' responsibility to formulate a purpose for the assembly's ministry, and to see that it is practically implemented. The elders will know whether the need is for exhortation, instruction, correction, evangelism and such-like. Similarly, they ought to be able to discern whether a series on a certain book, epistle or particular doctrine is most necessary at a given time. As shepherds, they will not only be aware of spiritual needs and "diet deficiencies," but will see to it that these are met, and met adequately.

A carefully prepared syllabus of subjects for ministry is extremely useful, and many assemblies have been literally revitalized by using one. In this connexion we should note that the elders of an assembly should feel perfectly free to ask an invited speaker to minister on a particular subject. They, after all, are the best guides (or should be) to the current needs of an assembly and to the Holy Spirit's leading within it. The generally accepted idea of leaving a speaker to be "led by the Spirit" to choose whatever subject he (as speaker) thinks fit for the occasion is not necessarily valid. Indeed, the Holy Spirit is quite likely to guide men whom He has appointed as overseers in the assembly concerning ministry-needs. We must never forget that it is a scriptural principle that spiritual guidance does not preclude intelligence, discretion and wise deliberation (I Cor. 14:32).

It is perhaps hardly necessary to point out that once a programme or syllabus has been agreed upon, this does not mean it is inflexible. Changes can and will be made by the assembly, which after all is a vital organism. However, once a plan has been formulated, it should at least be given a fair chance to succeed. The idea of casually disrupting a programme because a visiting speaker has unexpectedly appeared on the scene is not good. If the elders have given a plan due thought and launched it on a tide of prayer, then it should be implemented in positive fashion without vacillation.

ADEQUATE PROVISION

Some will object that it is one thing to formulate a purpose and draw up a programme, but another to discover personnel to make the thing go. There is plenty of room for scepticism if we base our thinking on "the way things are done at present." However, there are great possibilities if we will take another look and attempt a more thoughtful application of some broad, unchanging, scriptural principles.

There is no need to bring in an endless string of visiting speakers from all parts of the land to preach at our services. It is not only a wasteful policy economically and in terms of consuming the preacher's valuable time, but it is also unnecessary, not to say inefficient. It may come as a surprise to some to realise that while Mr. X may be a famous name "among us" and a good preacher, he is completely unknown to most of the folk in our neighbourhood whom we are trying to reach. Similarly, in the nature of the case, he is uninvolved in the problems of the lives and homes of the local believers and can have little or no pastoral concern for them. This is no reflection on the visitor; it is simply a factual representation of the case.

Recognizing the problem, let us look at some possible solutions. There are various ways in which the elders can provide for the teaching and edifying of the assembly. On the one hand they may decide to invite a suitably-gifted individual either from within the assembly or from outside it to minister consecutively on a shorter- or longer-term basis, without being in bondage to a calendar. Not only will this sharpen the preacher's ability in exposition, but also the congregation's desire for the Word expounded. Let us say at the outset for the sake of those who are haunted by the spectre of a "one-man ministry," that this proposal has absolutely nothing to do with clerisy. The elders will still function scripturally and responsibly. In any case it ought to be obvious that no one man, nor assembly for that matter, has a monopoly of gifts. This will be developed in the next chapter.

On the other hand, if the foregoing is not practicable, then several suitably-gifted individuals from within the assembly should be encouraged to participate. The great thing is to recognize that the criterion in deciding who shall minister is divine enduement. Elders should be on their guard against two popular opinions : first, the one that advocates "taking turns," and second, the one that suggests that "anybody can do it !" Scripture plainly teaches that the Risen Lord has given "gifts" to men, and "gifted men" to the church (cf. Eph. 4:8 f. with I Cor. 12), and confusion and barrenness result from overlooking this.

The doctrine of the priesthood of all believers emphasizes our complete equality, opportunity and responsibility in worship and approach to God. It does not mean that anyone should be allowed to minister in public at any time. The elders in an assembly will recognize capable men as well as undeveloped potential. They will realize that, while one man may be capable of a short series of talks, another may do well on a single occasion.

We ought to disabuse our minds of the idea that "local talent" is inferior. While it is often true that a prophet lacks honour at home, this sometimes indicates poor judgment on the part of those among whom the prophet lives rather than inability in the man himself. Perhaps it is a case of familiarity breeding contempt.

It should be noted here that a training-class for preachers and teachers can be invaluable both for individuals and for the assembly. Much more serious thought should be given to this aspect of the Christian education programme of any assembly.

Although little has been mentioned about it so far, we must recognize the importance of a definite spiritual exercise concerning ministry on the part of the elders themselves. If God has granted a man an enabling for ministry, he ought not to seek to escape from this responsibility. It is easy to say, "there are others who can do better" or, "I really am too busy;" but these are at best excuses, and often a thin veneer for false modesty. Many of the Lord's servants, especially those of a more retiring disposition, might wish to be silent, but the imperative of the divine call stirs them (see Jer. 1:4-10). There is always the danger of hiding our "pound" in a napkin.

If for some reason an assembly decides to import most of its speakers, there are still certain things that should be borne in mind. Variety may be the spice of life, but it can often be the ruin of an assembly. Visiting speakers should be given opportunity to present a series of messages rather than a "one-shot" sermon. Far better to have twelve speakers during the year taking one month each, than fifty-two different ones, or even one hundred and four! (where there are two preaching services each Sunday). A series of messages not only stimulates interest but adds perspective to the ministry. It would be ideal to arrange for several series under the one general syllabus planned by the elders.

We cannot over-emphasize the need for a more systematic and consecutive, expository-type ministry than we have become accustomed to. For too long we have been fed on a diet of textual and topical sermons, many very good in themselves, but quite unrelated, adding very little to the long-term effect of an assembly's ministry.

If this consecutive teaching programme sounds dull to people who have learned to survive on weekly or monthly "specials," then we can only plead that it be tried. There are completely new dimensions in a consecutive ministry. Not only will it help the congregation but it will be a tremendous stimulus to the preacher. It may not come easily the first few times, but perseverance will discover a new thrill and challenge in this scriptural way of handling the Scriptures. The preacher will discover new vistas, unlimited material and great freedom—to say nothing of not having to wonder "What shall I preach on next Sunday?"

Writing on the need to deal with "big themes" in our preaching, Dr. Jowett says:

And it ought to be that if men were to take only a square inch out of any of our preaching, they would find a suggestion which would lead them to 'the throne of God and of the Lamb.'

All this means that we must preach upon the great texts of the Scriptures, the fat texts, the tremendous passages whose vastnesses almost terrify us as we approach them. We may feel that we are but pygmies in the stupendous task, but in these matters it is often better to lose ourselves in the immeasurable than to always confine our little boat to the measurable creeks along the shore. Yes, we must grapple with the big things, the things about which our people will hear nowhere else; the deep, the abiding, the things that permanently matter. We are not appointed merely to give good advice, but to proclaim good news.[1]

[1] J. H. Jowett, *The Preacher; His Life and Work*, p. 100.

Nine

The Pastoral Ministry

> *"And he gave some to be apostles; and some, prophets; and some, evangelists; and some, pastors and teachers; for the perfecting of the saints unto the work of ministering, unto the building up of the body of Christ; till we all attain unto the unity of the faith, and of the knowledge of the Son of God, unto a fullgrown man, unto the measure of the stature of the fulness of Christ: that we may be no longer children, tossed to and fro and carried about with every wind of doctrine by the sleight of men in craftiness, after the wiles of error; but speaking the truth in love, may grow up in all things into him, which is the head, even Christ"* (Eph. 4:11-15).

TODAY THERE ARE MANY CRITICS OF ASSEMBLIES, BUT few who offer constructive, positive solutions to meet our ineffectiveness. Undeniably, our basic need is for genuine, spiritual awakening, but there is also need for more purposeful planning, particularly in the field of pastoral ministry. Bearing this in mind, and in a spirit of Christian love and concern, we offer the following reflections.

THE SCRIPTURAL BASIS OF A PASTORAL MINISTRY

It is unfortunate, to say the least, that while priding

ourselves on the carrying out of New Testament principles and doing things "according to the pattern" we have sometimes overlooked one of the basic elements of God's plan for a local church : pastoral ministry. This does not reflect a deliberate dishonesty but a lurking fear of an autocratic, one-man rule. It represents the swing of the pendulum away from the erroneous concept of a sacerdotal ministry which regarded itself as sole possessor of pastoral and spiritual grace.

The concept of a pastoral ministry does not originate with the New Testament but is at least suggested in the Old Testament (cf. Jer. 3:15; 17:16; 23:4; Ezek. 34:23, etc.). It is interesting to note in these Old Testament contexts that while the Lord condemns the false pastors He does not repudiate a pastoral ministry. He promises new shepherds, and even hallows such ministry by associating it with Messiah Himself. Granted, these terms may have a special connotation in the Old Testament, yet it cannot be denied that there is a foreshadowing of the gift of pastor which will find development in the New Testament.

In the New Testament, we must first of all consider the ministry of Paul in the early church. No doubt his ministry was unique and of a different order from that of the present-day pastor. However, this is not to deny the fact that in his work there are certain, significant principles discernible, which are of abiding value. Although Paul travelled so widely and viewed the world as his parish, he was willing to devote extended periods of ministry to local areas. He recognized that sometimes a more resident, pastoral ministry was in the divine plan.

Paul stayed a year and six months in the city of Corinth, in accordance with a specific divine revelation, "teaching the word of God among them" (Acts 18:11). At Ephesus he stayed even longer, and his three-year stay in that city covered almost the entire "Third Missionary Journey." A moment's reflection on his words to the Ephesian elders at Miletus reveals the nature of Paul's pastoral ministry (Acts 20:18-20, 31). In this statement Paul refers to some of the characteristic features of a pastor's work : consecutive exposition of Scripture and scriptural doctrines, public ministry, and visitation. The tears of both Paul and the Ephesians bespeak a pastoral ministry faithfully discharged.

The Pastoral Epistles take this type of ministry for granted. Timothy was clearly charged with pastoral ministry as an apostolic delegate at Ephesus. This ministry was fulfilled in conjunction with properly qualified and recognized elders who were themselves responsible, under God, for the spiritual well-being and government of the local church. There was no conflict of purpose or interest (II Tim. 2:2; I Tim. 4:14). As far as Titus was concerned the field of ministry lay in the island of Crete. His task was very similar to Timothy's (Titus 1:5). Both men were responsible to see that elders were appointed and that suitably-gifted men were trained and taught so that they in turn could teach others.

Writing concerning the gifts of the triumphant, risen Christ to the Church, Paul says :

> And he gave some to be apostles; and some, prophets; and some, evangelists; and some, pastors and teachers; for the perfecting of the saints unto the work of ministry unto the building up of the body of Christ (Eph. 4:11-12).

It is generally accepted that "apostles" here represents the founder-leaders of the Early Church, and "prophets" those who in those early times, prior to the completion of the Canon of Scripture, who were the media of revelation. The evangelists and pastor-teachers (these two words are best read together) represent the ministries which were not only exercised in the primitive church but are timeless functions linking the apostolic times with all other times. In other words, while the offices of apostle and prophet might be viewed as temporary and initatory, those of evangelist and pastor-teacher are more permanent and universal. The "evangelist" probably represents a pioneer ministry aimed at introducing people to Christ. The "pastor-teacher" is resident and his ministry more confirmatory. The whole purpose of this ministry is towards Christian maturity, which will itself be manifested in general participation in service and edification. This seems to be the particular point of Paul's repeated use of the preposition *eis* ("unto") in Eph. 4:12-13. One thing leads to another! To view the "pastor-teacher" as gifted to the Church at large does not materially alter Paul's meaning.

Before leaving this particular passage two interpretative comments may be noted. Westcott writes:

> The three groups 'apostles', 'prophets', 'evangelists', represent ministers who had charge not confined to any congregation or district. In contrast with these are those who form the settled ministry, 'pastors and teachers', who are reckoned as one class not from a necessary combination of the two functions but from their connection with a congregation.[1]

Bruce writes:

> The first two gifts are 'apostles' and 'prophets', both these terms to be understood in the sense which they bear in Ephesians 2:20 and 3:5. In our note on Ephesians 2:20 it was suggested that the 'foundation of the apostles and prophets' there is a reference to the apostles and prophets of the first Christian generation, who formed the Lord's foundation-gifts to His Church. . . . The second pair of gifts, evangelists and pastor-teachers (or teaching pastors), are required in each generation. . . . The two terms 'pastors (shepherds) and teachers' denote one and the same class of men. They are the men who 'tend the flock of God' and care for its wellbeing, showing other Christians by precept and example alike the path of Christian faith and life (I Peter 5:2; Acts 20:28). They are the same people as are elsewhere called elders and bishops, one of whose qualifications is being 'apt to teach' (I Timothy 3:2).[2]

[1] *Commentary on the Epistle to the Ephesians*, p. 62.
[2] *The Epistle to the Ephesians*, p. 85.

HISTORICAL PRECEDENT

It is interesting to remember that the Brethren Movement was originally something of a protest against organized Christianity as well as a positive, experimental step toward a visible expression of the oneness of the Body of Christ. However, although objecting to narrow sectarianism, and the unscriptural idea that the "minister" was alone qualified to dispense the elements at the Lord's Supper, the early Brethren did not object to a full-time pastoral, teaching ministry in an assembly. For them colloquially speaking that would have been "throwing out the baby with the bath water." Whatever measure of recognition they were or were not accorded, responsible individuals functioned as pastor-teachers. Here lay one of the secrets of the movement's early spiritual success, that there were divinely equipped (not to mention well-trained) men who were able to sustain an expository and pastoral ministry. At least passing reference should be made to the ministries of such as Robert Chapman at Barnstaple, Benjamin Wills Newton at Plymouth, George Müller and Henry Craik at Teignmouth and Bristol, Henry Heath at Woolpit and Henry Groves at Kendal. Clearly these early Brethren saw no conflict between their ministry and the real doctrine of the priesthood of all believers. Reference is made to this historical situation not in an attempt to seek the support of tradition, but to demonstrate the fallacy of the argument that the early Brethren refused to recognize a full-time pastoral ministry. For all their emphasis on simplicity and a Spirit-endued ministry, they still valued the proper exercise of pastoral gift.

PRACTICAL ADVANTAGES

The advantages of a settled, pastoral ministry are numerous and among the most outstanding are the following :

(i) It provides opportunity for a consecutive, expository, Bible-teaching ministry in which wide areas of Scripture can be treated in a systematic manner. Matters of Christian doctrine and behaviour can be dealt with as they occur in the inspired text of Scripture. Subjects that are often neglected because of their delicacy will come up for consideration more naturally, and there will therefore be no impugning the preachers' motive.

This consecutive type of ministry also encourages a more intelligent approach to the Bible. It enables the preacher to present truth contextually. We cannot expect to teach or edify on the basis of "one-shot sermons," which frequently are unrelated and disconnected. This is not to deny the value of an individual sermon, preached on an isolated occasion, but rather to point out the greater value of a straightforward, sustained, progressive exposition of Scripture. This will involve a number of other things, such as hard work and orderly study on the part of the preacher, but these are good too !

Furthermore, an expository, consecutive preaching tends to sharpen both the skill of the preacher and the spiritual discernment of the hearers. It is remarkable to see how people acquire a taste for this kind of preaching, and consequently for the Book upon which it is based. People can become all too easily discouraged by an apparently haphazard ministry, which for all its "inspiration" is not God's plan. How often we have settled for the type of arrangement where this week the message may be from Genesis and the next from Revelation. There are some who will take up the cudgels to defend this erratic type of ministry on the basis that it leaves room for the guidance of the Spirit. This is doubtful, however, since it is unlikely that the Spirit who inspired the sacred Manual will work counter to the method He therein prescribed for its exposition. We must remember that Scripture determines the preacher's method, as well as his message (Isa. 28:10, 13; II Tim. 4:2; Acts 20:27; I Cor. 14:30).

(ii) Another distinct advantage of a more continuous, preaching ministry is that through a prolonged contact between speaker and hearers the ministry becomes more related to the needs of the congregation. It is surprising how effective preaching can be when born not only of a sense of the sovereign Spirit's direction, but of an intimate, first-hand knowledge of the burdens and trials of a familiar congregation.

This local contact works both ways. It not only makes the preaching relevant but also inspires confidence in the hearers. In addition, if people are assured of a consistent and ordered ministry of the glorious Gospel they will be far more likely to bring visitors and friends. There is a justifiable hesitation to expose "contacts" and neighbours to something which is an unknown quantity.

(iii)   Another obvious advantage of a prolonged pastoral contact is the ministry of visitation. It is one of the tragic things of our age that there is so little care or concern for other people. Add to this the extreme involvement of our modern way of life, and it is little wonder that as far as so many assemblies are concerned there is little or no visitation. Visitation has a dual role in the life of a local church. It is fruitful in terms of fellowship and spiritual development, and in personal evangelism and outreach. There can be no denying the overseers' responsibility in this field as noted earlier, but here is a practical problem which requires more time than most busy men have in our contemporary, social structure. There are the physically and mentally sick, the aged and dying, those seeking marriage counsel, those with domestic and family problems, as well as seekers after truth. This takes time, not to say experience and preparation.

The right man, chosen of God and gifted for this ministry, can do much for a Christian community. He will be known as a man who treasures and guards confidences and people will be glad to unburden their hearts to a true pastor. There will ever be a strong reserve to "tell all" to the man who only has a casual contact, and is too busy for any other. The pastor listens, and although sometimes shocked and appalled by what he hears he must be able to advise and counsel. He can only do this effectively, if aware of his own weakness he casts himself on God, and takes time.

(iv) At the risk of being misunderstood, it must also be pointed out that bereft of any real, visible evidence of a full-time pastoral ministry our assemblies can present an unusual front to the world. A church without proper pastoral care is like a school without a teacher in the eyes of our contemporaries; and being eyed with suspicion we will find it more difficult to win our neighbours. We are not of course advocating conformity to a pattern prescribed by the world, but rather appealing for a fresh appraisal of scriptural possibilities and their translation into practical effect.

ACCEPTED ALTERNATIVES

Let us now consider some of the alternatives to a pastoral ministry, that we have come to accept.

(i) Perhaps we have run so far from the spectre of "one-man ministry" that we have settled for an "any man from anywhere ministry". We must, it seems, at all costs provide variety, and voice our protest against a supposed one-man ministry. We may even find the anomalous situation where a secretary is at pains to fill the church diary, even if he empties the pews!

(ii) We have settled all too often for a spasmodic and irregular outreach programme, instead of consistent and planned visitation. It is surprising what inventive genius is employed to devise means of contacting the neighbourhood, without work.

(iii) While discussing accepted alternatives, perhaps we should look briefly at the familiar pattern of the occasional visit of the "full-time", itinerant preacher. His coming and campaign are often viewed as the panacea for all that ails some inefficiently operating assembly. Although a stranger, he is expected to visit homes, preach stirring sermons, arouse sinners and console the saints—in short, perform miracles! The people who attend the special services will become acquainted with the visiting preacher and used to his approach. Then because of "our way of doing things", the preacher must leave and go elsewhere. The majority of the contacts are lost, and the same old routine-variety resumed. Another aspect of this arrangement, so often over-looked, is the problem of the travelling preacher's family. Does it really concern anyone that he is away from home more than he is there? Is anyone interested in the practical problem which constantly faces his family? The answers may be more glib than realistic. We are told that leaving the family is part of the sacrifice involved in a preacher's life. Is this really true? If so, there are some other questions that must be answered. For example, having established the pattern of home and family life, has God subsequently arranged church life and Christian service on lines which make family life impossible for His servants? Again, are preachers' children singled out for such neglect, that through lack of parental presence and paternal discipline and example they rebel against the Gospel and walk the road to perdition? Let it be clearly understood that these godly men are willing to make the sacrifice of home and family for the Lord's sake. However, is this really neces-sary? Is there no more scriptural pattern of ministry than this? As one peripatetic teacher put it : "It is not that I am unwilling to make the sacrifice, but I am not convinced that this is best for the assemblies in any case!"

POPULAR OBJECTIONS

Of the more serious popular objections to this type of resident, pastoral ministry we must take account of the following (we will first state the objection and then suggest an answer) :

(i) *The recognition of this type of arrangement will lead to a one-man ministry.*

In seeking to answer this objection we must first define terms. By "one-man ministry," the objector envisages a situation where one man becomes head of an assembly and takes over both the rule and oral teaching ministry. We strenuously deny that a scriptural form of the pastoral ministry even tends in this direction. The pastor is simply the servant of Christ in the local church and his presence in no way alters the status, responsibility, or pastoral concern of the recognized elders. Indeed it will be precisely the elders' desire to feed and shepherd "the flock in which the Holy Spirit has made them overseers" that will make room for a gifted pastor-teacher.

Christ is the undisputed Head and it is only a mischievous ecclesiology which disputes this. There is no sense in which the pastor is superior to any member of the body of Christ. A continuous, consecutive ministry in one locality does not mean the exclusion of all other gifts. In fact, there is sometimes more development of local gift in some so-called "denominational" churches than in some assemblies.

To suggest that a pastoral ministry necessarily means a one-man ministry is inaccurate. It would be humanly impossible for one man to take over all the ministries or services of the church. There is no disputing the fact that a New Testament pattern means total personnel involvement in the ministry or service of a local church. The New Testament illustration of a body in which each part plays its particular function makes this fact plain. However, this does not mean that every church member is divinely qualified, or should be allowed to take part, for example, in a public service. The ministries of the members are complementary not contradictory (cf. I Cor. 12:17-18). Far from producing a one-man ministry, a pastoral ministry should tend to encourage and train every man for service.

(ii) *A pastoral ministry is a denial of the doctrine of the priesthood of all believers.*

This sounds like a serious objection, but a moment's reflection reveals that it is not valid. All truly evangelical churches subscribe to this important scriptural doctrine. Indeed, this was one of the great recoveries of the Reformation. This is not a distinctly "Brethren" doctrine, as is obvious if we consider its meaning. The doctrine of the priesthood of all believers as we have seen teaches that, whereas under the Old Covenant the priesthood was limited to the chosen family of Aaron, under the New Covenant all believers are priests and have equally and without distinction the privilege of approach to God in worship. There is not now a privileged élite holding exclusive right of access. All God's people stand on common ground, their eligibility as worshippers being guaranteed by the precious blood of Christ.

Now a pastoral ministry in no way militates against this doctrine. There is no suggestion of the pastor being specially qualified to act before God. He will readily acknowledge that he has no special authority to "administer the sacraments" as some high churchmen teach. The scriptural view of the function of a pastor in no way conflicts with the idea of every believer's full privilege and responsibility to function in worship as a priest.

(iii) *There is a danger of producing lazy people and stifling local gift.*

Here again is a serious objection, if valid. That there are lazy people, and sometimes little exercise of local gift, cannot be denied. However, since this is the situation already prevailing, we cannot make a proposed pastoral ministry the scapegoat. Our contention is that if the pastor is allowed to fulfil his God-given task this particular situation will in fact soon be reversed, and a sermon-tasting, spoon-fed, congregation will be triggered into participation and activity. Far from stifling gift and encouraging laziness, this type of ministry will serve to reactivate the indolent and sharpen local gift. This does not mean that the pulpit will become a practice ground. On the other hand it does mean that definite steps will be taken to train and equip young men and others to "stir up the gift that is within them."

Some of those who raise this objection seem unaware of the present prevailing situation in many assemblies. They react violently against what they thoughtlessly call a "one-man ministry," yet lend their support to a system which continually imports different speakers from "all over the

globe." There is no exercise of local gift because every
week there is a different visiting preacher. Far from ex-
cluding all other gifts, pastoral ministry can even become
more fruitful in terms of developing gift in an assembly.

(iv) *If this arrangement is accepted it will lead to
clerisy.*

This objection has already been met, but some further
observations may be necessary. The distinction between
the clergy and the laity is often stressed in order to support
a sacerdotal ministry which believes itself to be sole possessor of spiritual grace. Clearly in this context, we are
not advocating such a distinction. A spiritual, pastoral
ministry will not differentiate between the grace resident in
one man and that in another. This objection is based on a
lack of information concerning the meaning of clerisy.
Without becoming involved in semantics, it may be
relevant to observe that the term "layman" has a much
wider connotation than our objector recognizes. Broadly
speaking, a layman is a man who is other than an expert
in a particular field. Bearing this in mind, it is evident that
while most men are laymen in the field of oral ministry or
even pastoral ministry, there are others who are more
expert. There is no ground for calling these experts the
"clergy." They are simply "servants (*diakonoi*) through
whom ye believed, and each as the Lord gave to him"
(I Cor. 3:5 RV). Evangelicalism, generally, acknowledges
the dangers of clerisy, but because we recognize the dangers
it does not follow that we walk blindly into them!

(v) *This would undermine the "faith principle"
generally accepted among assembly workers.*

Here is another objection which is more an appeal to
prejudice than an honest appraisal of facts. We are not
here discussing the validity or otherwise of the traditional
method of financial support of the ministry among assemblies, though there might be ample scope for such discussion. After all it is only one of several possibilities. There
is no need for an assembly to enter into a financial contract
or pay a salary to a pastor. If they and he prefer a more

flexible arrangement, this can be easily worked out. Moreover, it is surprising how an assembly will be able to meet the financial responsibility involved in maintaining a full-time worker, if it accepts the divine plan of giving. The idea of financial support for ministry given, is clearly a New Testament principle (cf. I Cor. 9:4-14).

Paul writes to Timothy:

> Let the elders that rule well be counted worthy of double honour, especially those who labour in the word and in teaching. For the scripture saith, Thou shalt not muzzle the ox when he treadeth out the corn. And, The labourer is worthy of his hire (I Tim. 5:17-18).

These words envisage financial support of local ministry. The word "honour" (*timēs*) as noted earlier might be translated "honorarium" (cf. W. E. Vine, *Expository Dictionary of N.T. Words*). This passage obviously recognizes the possibility of a man's devoting part or even all of his time to a local ministry. As an elder he shows special aptitudes and exercises a pastoral ministry. The name is unimportant providing the job is done.

(vi) *This could easily lead to a man dominating the assembly.*

There is no real reason why the recognition of a pastoral ministry in an assembly should result in the assembly being dominated by one man. After all, as pointed out earlier, the pastor is primarily a servant of the Lord in the church, and as such he will seek to guide but not to dominate. Those of us who have spent our lives in assembly fellowship and have some kind of concern for it, have sometimes been amazed at the Diotrephes-spirit and domineering of some totally incapable men. It might well be that the presence of a spiritual pastor in an assembly would prevent this type of situation rather than aggravate it.

Other points might doubtless be raised with regard to this subject, though we believe that none of these difficulties would prove insurmountable. Suffice it to say that we are not suggesting that the recognition of a more settled pastoral ministry would solve all assembly problems. This is no panacea. However, it is time that some more positive, prayerful thinking be engaged in on the whole topic of the pastoral care of the local church. Out of such thought might come some clear direction from the Lord as to the best way to implement such convictions. What is done to meet the need may differ, according to the area, circumstances or spiritual conditions.

A pastoral ministry will also help in communication. Strange though it may seem, in this age of cybernetic wonders, we are so often confronted with the problem of communication. Local churches are not exempt from this problem, in fact in some, where organization is suspect, it is aggravated. Sometimes, admittedly, it is a failure to grasp the significance of the information available or perhaps a lack of concern to share it with others, but more often than not it results from a lack of channels.

Now where an assembly has the advantage of a resident worker with a well equipped office and telephone, it is surprising how co-ordination of effort and communication of information can be achieved. This does not mean that the man is to be bogged down with all the necessary paper work and minutiae that go to make a church tick, but it does mean that there is someone available with time to help facilitate the functioning of the group. Such matters as : keeping in touch with the sick and needy and tactfully bringing these people's problems before the church; sharing suitable prayer requests; mentioning missionary problems; answering emergency calls; co-ordinating the church calendar and scheduling activities, are all important and can be handled more efficiently if there is some focal point of reference. There may well be committees for handling specific areas of the church's life and ministry, and it is good to involve as many as possible in the stewardship of responsibility, but there must be co-ordination, and this is where a local worker may be a great help, providing of course he be accorded a reasonable degree of responsibility and freedom.

For example, if an assembly feels it is too small to seek the advantages of the ministry of a resident servant of Christ, there are still possibilities open. It may well be that there are other local churches who would value some assistance in visitation and ministry. Several churches could work together and perhaps invite one of the Lord's servants to come and reside in their general locality. In this way his ministry would then be available as would his time, and this might well not only stimulate greater effort but effect closer fellowship between the co-operating assemblies.

Of course there are limitations to this kind of arrangement. Obviously the burden of such a work could become heavy for one worker and local brethren would need to be graciously considerate and helpful. The scheduling of meetings would need to be carefully worked out so that the advantages of consecutive ministry could still be enjoyed. Due consideration being given to these problems, there are still wonderful possibilities. We can only hope and pray that those who have a genuine care for God's people will seek to be sensitive so that they, like the children of Issachar, may be men that have understanding of the times to know what Israel (or today, the Lord's people) ought to do (I Chron. 12:32).

Ten

Deacons in the New Testament

> ". . . men of good report, full of the Spirit and of wisdom" (Acts 6:3).
> ". . . let these also first be proved; then let them serve as deacons, if they be blameless" (I Tim. 3:10).

DEACON-WORK, LIKE CHRISTIAN SERVICE OF ANY KIND, is a practical expression of the faith once delivered to the saints. While the preaching of the Word of God and the proper care of the people of God are vital to the effective life of a local church, these are not alone. The consistent, careful work of godly deacons is indispensable, and although often carried out behind the scenes is accepted before God as of great price.

There is always the danger of thinking that because this type of service relates to the ordinary and mundane it is of less consequence. We ought to remember that a cup of cold water offered in Christ's name is of greater worth than a silver chalice raised in perfunctory fashion at a Mass. The Psalmist speaking on behalf of one of the Levites who was apparently temporarily indisposed says: "I had rather be a door-keeper in the house of my God, than to dwell in the tents of wickedness" (Ps. 84:10). This is the true spirit of a deacon.

It is a principle in Christian service that faithfulness in little things qualifies a man for responsibility in bigger things. Worldly values are so inverted, and we as Christians are often unfortunately prone to adopt them. We may therefore miss the blessing that necessarily accrues from doing "whatever we do heartily as unto the Lord."

There is need of many things in the churches today, as in any age, not least among them people of high principle and genuine love for Christ who will serve Him and His people. What more noble task could we ask than the privilege of serving the King of kings in establishing His kingdom on earth and in the lives of men? It is in fact sharing His "easy yoke" of service.

With these thoughts in mind, we turn now to the whole field and ministry of deacons.

While considerable emphasis has been placed on the subject of eldership and sincere attempts have been made to give practical expression to this matter in the government of local churches, very little comparatively speaking has been said about the appointment and ministry of deacons. This is certainly an important subject and its neglect must surely have a deleterious effect upon the smooth functioning of a local church in day-to-day affairs and matters of practical import.

THE WORD "DEACON"

The English term "deacon" is derived from the Greek word *diakonos* which it practically transliterates. *Diakonos* although used thirty times in the Greek New Testament is translated "deacon" only three times in the AV (Phil. 1:1; I Tim. 3:8, 10). The two other occurrences of the word "deacon" in the Authorised text represent *diakoneō* (a cognate of *diakonos*) in the original. It may be noted that in the AV *diakonos* is rendered "minister" twenty times and "servant" seven times.

Originally a *diakonos* was a servant who waited at table, and this idea is never far from the surface when the word and its cognates (*diakoneō* and *diakonia*) are used in the

New Testament. We may safely say that, although in some New Testament occurrences these terms suggest a pastoral or preaching ministry, generally speaking they indicate practical ministration in material matters.

That *diakonos* came to have a sort of technical meaning in the second half of the first century of Christianity is obvious from the use and context in the four places where it is translated "deacon" in the AV. However, we must be careful to recognize that, however developed or otherwise this technical usage of the word may have been in New Testament days, the emphasis in Scripture is placed unquestionably upon the work of a deacon rather than on his office and title. While we must derive all the help we can from specific scriptural references, we must be careful not to read back into the text concepts with which we are familiar today or technicalities which are not really there. As F. F. Bruce remarks,

> It is an anachronism to apply to New Testament persons and conditions names which have acquired a stereotyped ecclesiastical sense. The New Testament has, generally speaking, no *technical* vocabulary for functions in the churches and for those who discharge them but uses ordinary Greek words, which had best be rendered by ordinary English words.[1]

NEW TESTAMENT TEACHING

While some have sought a derivation of the New Testament diaconate in the service of the Chazzan (synagogue attendant) in Judaism, or in that of the cult official (to whom the term *diakonos* was applied) of Hellenistic paganism, it seems best to recognize with J. B. Lightfoot[2] that this particular ministry was new with Christianity. It grew out of a specific need and developed within the life of the early churches. Evidently it became somewhat regularized and organized so that by the time Paul wrote his Pastoral Epistles he was able to discuss the necessary qualifications for deaconship.

[1] *The Acts of the Apostles*, 2nd ed., p. 152.
[2] cf. *Philippians*, essay on "The Christian Ministry."

The starting point in any discussion of the subject of deacons in the New Testament must necessarily be Luke's description of the appointment of the seven almoners in Acts 6. Their appointment resulted from a dispute between two main segments of the Jerusalem church. The Greek-speaking, Jewish Christians were not satisfied that their widows were receiving adequate support from the common fund which had originally been established as a tangible expression of fellowship in the Jerusalem church. They felt that the Aramaic-speaking Jews, the more conservative element in the church, were taking an unfair advantage. In order to prevent a spread of ill-feeling, which would certainly have ruined the effectiveness of the church, the apostles wisely called a church meeting and presented a satisfactory solution to the difficulty.

They suggested the appointment of a seven-man body to administer financial affairs. Although they might have handled this matter themselves, the apostles decided that it would be wrong for them to become further burdened with the everyday affairs of the church when there were perfectly capable individuals available to help. The church gladly acquiesced, and selected seven men who were then duly appointed by the apostles.

The seven men appointed were all of the Greek-speaking party, judging from their names, and one, Nicolas of Antioch, was evidently a gentile convert to Judaism. Only two of the seven figured prominently again in the story of the Early Church; they were Stephen and Philip. It was not simply politics that dictated the nomination and appointment of these seven Hellenists for, as Luke faithfully records, they had to meet certain basic requirements before they could be accepted. They were to be church members in good standing whose integrity was beyond question, and men who were full of the Holy Spirit and wisdom.

The actual responsibility committed to these men who were later known as "the Seven" (Acts 21:8) is summarized in two phrases used by the apostles; they were to "serve tables" (*diakonein trapezais*) and be "over this business" (*epi tēs chreias tautēs*). Combining these phrases we see that the seven were specifically appointed to office in order to administer the material affairs of the Jerusalem church, particularly in matters of finance.

It is important to recognize further that their ministry, although complementary, was distinct from and in contrast with that of the apostles, who were now free to become involved exclusively in the regular prayer and preaching ministry of the church. However, it is evident from the effective ministries of Stephen, the apologist and first Christian martyr, and Philip the evangelist, that no limitation was placed upon the "Seven", nor were they precluded from oral ministry.

Some commentators see no connexion between this incident in Acts 6 and the order of deacons found later in the New Testament. In defence of this position they point out that the word "deacon" is not used by Luke in his narrative and that he gives no hint of their being other than almoners. It should be noted, however, that while the actual noun *diakonos* is not used its cognate verb *diakoneō* is (v. 2), as well as the substantive *diakonia* (v. 1). Furthermore, while it may be true that the immediate situation called for almoners, there is no need to limit the phrase *diakonein trapezais* to "handing out dole." Almost certainly this phrase is used metaphorically and is an attempt on the part of the apostles to point out the difference between the administration of mundane matters and the handling of spiritual decisions and oral ministry. In any case, even if the "Seven" began as almoners only, it is obvious that their writ would quickly widen to embrace all sorts of other matters, especially with an expanding church such as the one in Jerusalem. Indeed, it is relevant to note that this organized and capable administration led to even greater expansion, including the conversion of some of the Jewish priests (v. 7).

J. B. Lightfoot who assumes "that the office thus established represents the later diaconate" and cannot see "how

the identity of the two can reasonably be called in question," points out that : "it seems clear from the emphasis
with which St. Luke dwells on the new institution, that he
looks on the establishment of this office, not as an isolated
incident, but as the initiation of a new order of things in
the Church" (*Philippians*, p. 188).

He also points out that earliest Christian tradition identified the "Seven" as deacons. Irenaeus, a disciple of
Polycarp who was in turn a disciple of the Apostle John,
distinctly refers to these men as "deacons" in his writings.

There are several other New Testament passages which
relate to the subject of deacons. The one dealing with it
most fully is Paul's first pastoral letter to Timothy (see
I Tim. 3 :8-13). We shall deal with this later when examining the qualifications of a deacon. It is important to see
that Paul is just as concerned about the recognition and
appointment of "deacons" as he is of "elders" or "overseers." He evidently recognized the legitimacy and value
of their function in the Christian churches.

This passage in Timothy is also important in that it
provides for the ministry of deaconesses, if this is the
meaning of *gynaikas hōsautōs* in v. 11. In defence of this
interpretation we should notice that if Paul had intended
us to understand his reference to indicate deacons' wives,
as in the AV, he would almost certainly have used *tas
gynaikas autōn*. The Revisers render it quite ambiguously
"women." We know from a reference in Paul's final
chapter to the Romans that there were women like Phoebe
of Cenchrea, who worked as "deaconesses" in the church.
Judging from the context and language employed, Phoebe
may well have been engaged on some deaconess "rescue-
mission-assignment" when she visited Rome. This would
explain why Paul was anxious to solicit the co-operation
of the church in her enterprise (Rom. 16:1-2, cf. mg.).

We know that there were deaconesses in the post-New
Testament era of the Church and the Greek Fathers regularly read *gynaikas* in this sense in I Tim. 3:11. If it be
argued that Paul is simply referring to deacons' wives in

this context, then it seems strange that such qualifying demands be made of them when none were made of the wives of the "overseers" (*episkopoi*). No doubt the need for deaconesses was partly dictated by the social conditions of the New Testament era, when women were kept in seclusion and men would be quite unable to gain access or offer assistance to them. It is interesting to observe how often procedures were established among the early Christians on the basis of need and opportunity. For this very reason, while not necessarily bound by the customs and practices of the New Testament era, we can learn from them, at the same time seeking to discover basic principles which can be applied effectively at any age.

Another passage worthy of notice in this connexion is the salutation in Paul's epistle to the Philippians. Here he addresses himself to "all the saints in Christ Jesus which are at Philippi, with the bishops and deacons" (*sun episkopois kai diakonois*). It is evident that by this date (*c.* AD 62) the "officers" in the church were not only known but recognized as in a place of responsibility. While there was full co-operation between them, there was still evidently a clear demarcation between those who ruled in spiritual matters and those who conducted the everyday affairs of the assembly. We know from other references that the Philippian church was not only a generous and practically minded body, but also efficient in distributing its funds (Phil. 2:25-30, 4:10; II Cor. 8:1-5). It may be that their practical effectiveness was furthered by the faithful service of these whom Paul addresses as "deacons." Like their fellow-labourers, the overseers, the deacons evidently functioned collegiately. Although known within the church for their special ministry, there is no suggestion here that the deacons had unique secular qualifications, or for that matter distinct spiritual privileges, that would tend to ecclesiastical preference. They stood on common ground with all the believers, but were gifted and recognized as such to fulfil a specific function.

Before proceeding to a discussion of deacons' qualifications, there are two passages to which brief reference should be made. One is Rom. 12:17 and the other I Pet. 4:11. In the former Paul is stressing the importance of all the complementary functions of the different members of the body of Christ. This catalogue of "gifts" includes "ministry" (v. 7). He writes ". . . or ministry (*diakonian*) let us wait on our ministering (*en tē diakonia*)." While this might be construed in the general sense of service, it is possible that Paul has in mind some more specific responsibility and its exercise. This seems specially likely since *diakonia* comes between prophecy (*prophēteia*—forthtelling) and teaching (*didaskalia*).

In I Pet. 4:10-11 we have a similar emphasis. The Apostle is exhorting his readers to use their God-given gift (*charisma*) as "good stewards of the manifold (*poikilēs*— lit. "variegated") grace of God." He then elaborates and mentions two specific areas of charismatic exercise, speaking and ministering (*diakonein*). Probably, though not necessarily, Peter had in mind the elders' and the deacons' functions respectively. He becomes more specific about the former later in his epistle (see I Pet. 5:1-4).

Some see a deacon ministry referred to in Paul's term "helps" (*antilēpseis*) used in I. Cor. 12:28. This is open to question, especially since the word employed is capable of very wide application.

Eleven

The Character, Ministry and Encouragement of Deacons

> *And the charge of the sons of Gershon in the tent of meeting shall be the tabernacle and the Tent, the covering thereof, and the screen for the door of the tent of meeting, and the hangings of the court, and the screen for the door of the court, which is by the tabernacle, and by the altar round about, and the cords of it for all the service thereof* (Num. 3:25, 26).

A DEACON'S QUALIFICATIONS ARE CLEARLY SET FORTH IN I Tim. 3:8-12. First Paul suggests seven "personal" requirements and then two "domestic" ones. As in the case of the qualifications for overseership, which incidentally are more numerous and if anything more onerous, some of these requirements seem somewhat elementary. In examining them, however, we must remember the background of the age in which these pastoral letters were written. It may be best if we deal with these matters in the order in which they occur in the text, rather than attempt to classify them.

PERSONAL QUALIFICATIONS (I Tim. 3:8-10)

(i) "Grave" (*semnos*). This word conveys more the idea of respect and dignity than a forbidding sternness. The cognate noun *semnotēs* is used in I Tim. 2:2 where the AV translates it "honesty" and the RSV "respectful in every way." It seems that *semnos* has more to do with a man's attitude of heart and set of values than a disapproving look on his face. The NEB translates it helpfully "men of high principle." A deacon will have such a sense of the will of God for his life and such an awareness of true Christian principle that he will not only show respect but will earn it from others.

(ii) "Not double-tongued" (*dilogos*). This is the only occurrence of the word in the New Testament. Its cognate noun *dilogia* had the meaning "given to repetition" or "talebearing", but judging from our present context this adjective probably means "guilty of double talk" or "equivocal." A deacon's word must be dependable. He must have none of the characteristics of "Mr. Facing-both-ways." He must be a man of transparent sincerity.

(iii) "Not given to much wine." An addiction to "strong drink" must necessarily disqualify a man for deaconship, first because of its disgusting consequences, and second because of the nature of his task. In dealing with people and their problems, visiting their homes and meeting them in society, the deacon would be frequently exposed to temptation. If there was this danger in New Testament days, how much more so in our contemporary society with its social drinking and inevitable cocktail parties!

(iv) "Not greedy of filthy lucre" (*mē aischrokerdeis*). Although this strange archaism of the AV is well known it is probably better to translate "not having an insatiable appetite for base gain." This does not proscribe making a reasonable profit in an honourable commercial pursuit. Rather does it prohibit an avid materialist from holding office. If a man is covetous there will be the danger of his being unscrupulous in dealing with others, to say nothing of using his office for personal advantage and pecuniary gain (Tit. 1:11). More than one church treasurer has fallen into the snare of Judas (John 12:6).

(v) "Holding the mystery of the faith in a pure conscience." There are two possible ways of interpreting this phrase. On the one hand it may mean that the deacon must tenaciously adhere to the articles of the Christian faith; on the other, that he must have personally appropriated the Christian revelation by faith. It seems best to understand the former meaning here, since a personal acceptance of Christ is a *sine qua non* for church membership, quite apart from deaconship. Paul is saying that the would-be deacon must not only be conscientious in the execution of his practical duties, but must also give evidence that in all good conscience he is aware of, and committed to, the essential doctrines of the Christian faith. It is not simply a lip-service orthodoxy but a genuine, inner conviction about fundamentals that is in view.

(vi) "And let these first be proved." Paul is not providing for a formal, written or oral examination for deacons (though this might not be a bad idea!) nor is he saying that a man must serve a long period of probation. His use of the verb *dokimazein* suggests rather the approbation of the church before a man is invited to serve. This is in keeping with the procedure described by Luke in Acts 6:3. If a man patently lacked the straightforward requirements for service in the local church, then he would be unacceptable. There is not the same emphasis here as in the word "novice" applied in verse 6 to the overseer. While a "new Christian" (which is essentially the meaning of *neophytos*) would be ineligible for eldership, it is not unreasonable that such a person, especially if his pre-Christian training and experience tended in this direction, might soon, having become grounded in the faith and given evidence of reality, be given the responsibility of deaconship.

(vii) "Blameless (*anenklētos*). This is probably to be linked in thought with what precedes. In other words, if a man having undergone the scrutiny of the church has emerged irreproachable, then he should forthwith be summoned to serve. Paul's words suggests the thought of "no charge against the man having been substantiated."

Domestic Qualifications (I Tim. 3:12)

As in the case of the elder, the deacon's family and home-life come in for examination before he can be appointed. The reason for such scrutiny is plainly stated in connexion with the overseer. His "rule" in the home will evidence his ability to rule in the church. While no specific reason for this "home test" is given in connexion with the deacon, it is fairly obvious why it would be necessary. Unless a man displayed some kind of discipline of mind and character, as well as ability to arrange his domestic affairs in an orderly manner, he is unlikely to be able to contribute much to "doing things decently and in order" in the church.

(i) "Let deacons be husbands of one wife." This regulation is not intended to disqualify single men or remarried widowers from the diaconate, but to stress the need for moral propriety in those who bear responsibility. In an age which condoned polygamy with all its heartbreak and attendant evils, it was essential for Christians to be on their guard. No man who favoured this idea could be allowed to serve in the church. Obviously a man who was a faithful deacon might sometimes be exposed to temptation. He must be of such strength of character and irreproachable morality that his reputation would not be impugned.

To strike a practical note here, it should be observed that a single man might frequently find his hands tied in attempting to deal with certain practical problems in an assembly. (Just as an unmarried elder might well be handicapped in this area of ministry.) For this reason, among many others, we detect much sanity in the Scriptures, which incidentally never hint that celibacy might better qualify a man for Christian service.

(ii) "Ruling their children and their own houses well." In Paul's day, as in our own, the best test of a man's integrity was his domestic behaviour. It is easy for a man to create a good public image yet be sadly deficient at home. Christianity knows no such double standard. It is concerned with what a man really is, not what he appears to be, especially if that man bears responsibility in the church. A well-ordered Christian home was, and still is, one of the best advertisements for Christianity in any community. Similarly, while a man will not ultimately be held responsible for the behaviour of his adult children, especially if they are obdurate and unbelieving, he is responsible for the conduct and discipline of his offspring while they are minors. The scandalous permissiveness and unkind indulgence of many Christian parents in our contemporary society is not only harmful to their children but also a sad reflection on the church of God. Plainly the man who is father of undisciplined children or the head of a disorganized household is unsuitable material for diaconate service.

While mentioning the deacon's qualifications, something should be said about the requirements for "women" in v. 11. As noted earlier, some refer these words to the deacons' wives (so AV). If this is the meaning, then the wife who would necessarily be involved with him in his work must evidence moral decorum, regulated speech, sobriety and faithfulness. It seems more likely (as noted earlier) that the persons in view here are deaconesses, but in any case the point is well made that the foregoing virtues become all who are involved in the Lord's service. Control of tongue, temper and appetite are good evidences of spiritual maturity.

Having reviewed these qualifications for deaconship, it is easy to see why the apostles suggested in the election of the "Seven" that they be "seven men of honest report, full of the Holy Ghost and wisdom" (Acts 6:3). A deacon, like an overseer, must be a man of considerable spiritual stature. Deaconship, like eldership, is no sinecure but will demand the utmost of a man and will quickly reveal his moral and spiritual fibre.

APPOINTMENT AND WORK OF DEACONS

While it must be said that appointing a man to an office does not guarantee his functioning effectively, we must recognize that the plain inference of the New Testament is that men were definitely appointed as deacons. It has been argued that the New Testament talks about deacon service rather than a diaconate. There is a modicum of truth in this, but both the Acts account of the appointment of the "Seven" and Paul's listing of deacon qualifications in the Pastoral Epistles suggest that there were certain individuals who were specifically recognized as deacons and functioned in that capacity. In Luke's narrative the men were nominated by the church and commissioned to the work by the apostles. There can be little doubt that subsequent to the death of the apostles the elders would have assumed the responsibility for appointing deacons.

Commenting on this matter. F. F. Bruce writes,

"The seven men in Acts 6 were nominated by the rank and file of the church and confirmed in office by the apostles. This may suggest how men may be selected for comparable service today, the elders (for this purpose) taking the place of the apostles."[1]

In a well-ordered local church of today, deacons should be appointed to serve only after due thought, prayer and teaching. On a suitable occasion the assembled church might be asked to nominate (preferably by secret ballot to avoid any embarrassment or misunderstanding) those from the company whom they consider to be suitably gifted and qualified for deacon service. Then, after due consultation and prayer and in the light of their intimate knowledge of the assembly, the elders should take steps to confirm the appointment of those suggested by the church. Ideally, the elders should have no difficulty in accepting the recommendations of the assembly, although for practical reasons there should be a limit on the number of men appointed. In order to encourage fellowship in this type of service to the assembly, it would probably be well to suggest a limited tenure of office. There need be nothing hard and fast about this. It would, however, not only prevent a man

[1] *A New Testament Church in 1955*, pp. 45 f.

becoming "too used" to a work and therefore losing his usefulness, but would also give opportunity to younger men whose gifts might otherwise be quenched. Perhaps two or three years might be a long enough term, except under unusual circumstances.

RELATION BETWEEN OVERSEERS AND DEACONS

While there are clear differences between the work of an overseer and that of a deacon they will work happily together and complement each other's ministry. We have seen that historically deacons were appointed that they might share the weight of responsibility devolving upon the apostles (and later, upon the elders). As the Jerusalem church grew numerically so did the problems, especially since the Christians were committed to a voluntary "welfare" programme. Eventually, the load became unwieldy for the apostles, and the deacons stepped in to help shoulder it.

There was never any thought of rivalry or competition between these groups since their areas of responsibility were clearly defined. The apostles gave themselves to the "ministry of the word and to prayer," while the deacons involved themselves in the day to day affairs of the church and dealt with practical matters. It is evident from Paul's address to the Philippians that the overseers and deacons were on the best of terms and were both recognized for the responsibility they bore. The juxtaposition of elder and deacon "qualifications" in the Pastorals suggests the same thing. It seems strange that in the light of this clear New Testament picture the church should have misunderstood. Today we have men called "deacons" who are doing the work of overseers and vice-versa. In some churches the word "deacon," strange to relate, is reserved for a man who has taken "holy orders" and regards himself as belonging to a distinct "clergy-class." Frequently in assemblies we have elders who are burdened down not only by their legitimate ministry as overseers, but also by the practical and more peripheral "chores" of deacons. In other words we have turned full circle back to the situation in which the apostles wisely appointed "deacons" in the first place. While there may be a legitimate, innate fear of top-heavy organization and the multiplication of office holders, we ought not to turn our back on scriptural principles and procedures as if irrelevant in this age. We can certainly learn much from the way the early church operated. Perhaps some elders feel they will lose their "grip" on the assembly by delegating responsibility to deacons. If this is their thinking, then maybe it is about time they did, and further, that they realized that an elder's influence in an assembly should be a spiritual one. Elders who think they are capable of handling deacon work as well are not only cultivating an attitude which is ultimately harmful to the assembly, but are also conditioning themselves for peptic ulcers.

There is little doubt that deacon work may be a sort of apprenticeship for eldership. A man who becomes involved in the practical workings of an assembly and the problems of people is quite likely to develop a "shepherd's heart." Such a man is invaluable and it is to be hoped that the elders will recognize him for what he has become—one of them!

By suggesting a distinction of their ministries we are not saying that elders and deacons should work independently. There should be the closest co-operation between them, but each group specializing in its own field. In a well-ordered assembly one of the elders would probably function as chairman of the deacons' meeting or, at least, provide definite liaison. Perhaps there might be an occasional joint meeting of elders and deacons. They should aways be on the best terms of fellowship, although their areas of responsibility are fairly clearly defined as different.

Spheres of Ministry

Any attempt at defining deacon work will be inadequate and must be regarded simply as tentative. In the practical working of an assembly the distinction between elders' and deacons' work will quickly become apparent. As noted earlier, the New Testament is not a rulebook but a revelation of spiritual principles which are universally applicable. Any attempt at definition here is made with a view to helping and guiding only. Here are some of the spheres in which deacons might function.

(a) Finance. We begin here, not because it is necessarily the most important area of deacon work, but because it was in this field that deacons first came into view. Obviously, those who care for the financial matters of an assembly must be men of unquestioned integrity. It was for this reason, no doubt, that the apostles laid down such stringent requirements for those who were "to serve tables" in the first place, as well as to silence an incipient scandal.

Anyone who is familiar with the workings of an assembly "oversight meeting," will know how much time can be consumed discussing finance. This is unfortunate because elders' time is at a premium, and in any case they are called to deal with other matters. While it may be true that the spiritual leaders of a local church should be concerned about practical matters such as the spiritual principles involved in the assembly's "giving," and "fellowship" with those engaged in Christian service, the actual distributing or almoner work belongs properly to the deacons. While this side of the deacon's work may be less onerous in these days of welfare societies and "medicare," there is still ample scope for spiritually alert and able men to "keep the books," and act as modern "Epaphroditi." It may well be that unrealistic attitudes to giving and the tragic lack of support of the ministry at home and overseas stem in part from our dispensing with the ministry of deacons. Irresponsibility in this, as in other matters, is contagious.

(b) Trusteeship. Here is another wide field of service for a deacon. Usually we see elders acting as trustees for assemblies and thus becoming involved in legal matters, building and equipment maintenance, and the minutiae of running a church. This is essential work and not only vital to the effectiveness of the church, but necessary from the point of view of the state and law. However, we submit that in the very nature of the case this is work for deacons, not elders. If it is argued that there might be matters of principle and church policy involved in trustee work, then the answer again lies in the proper qualification for deaconship. In any case, in this as in all other areas, the deacons will not work in "splendid isolation" from the overseers.

(c) *Visitation.* The only limit in this field is the one we may arbitrarily prescribe. A deacon who knows his calling and place in the church can be invaluable in establishing contacts through visitation. Of course, this is everyone's field of service, but it will need careful overseeing, planning and execution. Here is where the deacon comes in. He will concern himself to find out opportunities and contacts and see that they are carefully and systematically followed up. Even if it could be proved that "door to door visitation" is a thing of the past, and this is a moot point especially in the light of the notorious success of certain very undesirable modern religious elements, there are literally unlimited opportunities for visiting "fringe contacts." These are the parents of Sunday School children (who should also be visited by Sunday School teachers), neighbours, sometime-enquirers and visitors, and those people who have "come to church" on those special occasions.

The elders will, of course, be visiting the "flock" and seeking to establish pastoral contact, and so may be too busy to become involved in the "outreach" visitation programme. This is the field of deacons. Scripture makes provision for this and lays considerable stress upon the deacons' "social" qualifications, as noted.

(d) *Correspondence.* There is always considerable correspondence involved in the workings and ministry of a local church. Letters to speakers, to missionaries, to the authorities, to "shut-ins," and to members who are away from home. These are but a few. In a busy, larger assembly, secretarial work is practically a full-time job. A deacon who is a "ready scribe" could be worth his weight in gold. Why is it that in some circles "the correspondent" is regarded as the "top job," essentially belonging to an elder? It must have been one such "correspondent" who suggested the translation "secretary" for "angel" in each of the seven letters in the Apocalypse! Surely it is true of a "good elder," as of a good leader, that he is the man who has learned to delegate responsibility. When elders do the work of elders, and deacons that of deacons, it is surprising how the wheels turn and the loads are lightened. Other areas of deacon service are Sunday School work, social functions, publicity and advertising, platform arrangement, ushering, missionary contacts, and music.

If there are recognized deaconesses (and there seems at least some scriptural and historical support for their existence) then they could concern themselves with such matters as hospitality, sick visitation, and women's work in general.

PRACTICAL CONSIDERATIONS

In order for the ministry of deacons to be effective there are certain practical matters to keep in mind. First it is necessary for them to have a clearly defined field of service allocated to them. There is a real danger of anyone's job becoming no one's job. Sometimes it is useful if each deacon, always of course in fellowship with his colleagues, has a particular area of ministry given to him. If he is wise, he will spread the load and involve others, but essentially he is responsible to the elders, and in turn to the church, for one particular ministry.

This defining of responsibility is in no way to limit a man's service but to guarantee that jobs are done. As we saw in the story of the "Seven", while their ministry was defined, they were able to go far beyond it. For example, Stephen became an outstanding teacher and defender of the faith, while Philip was later to be known as "the Evangelist." Perhaps it was their faithfulness in "serving tables" that at least developed other latent talents. The shouldering of responsibility is one of the best means of strengthening a man's character and maturing him. "It is good for a man that he bear the yoke in his youth" (Lam. 3:27) is a sound principle, and one all too easily overlooked by some seniors who feel that to relinquish office is a sign of weakness. In fact, it is often an evidence of spiritual maturity and faith.

The regular convening of properly conducted deacons' meetings will also be necessary if these chosen men are to get things done. These meetings would afford opportunity for honest evaluation as well as concerted planning. There is nothing unspiritual about an agenda and the recording of minutes. Both will lend definition and depth to discussion and planning. The chairman should act as such and keep the meeting on the right lines. As suggested earlier, it might help to have one of the elders act as chairman of the deacons' meeting, so that there is complete rapport between those who minister and those who administer. In any case a report of the proceedings at the deacons' meeting should be presented to the elders who will then be kept advised of what is going on. Even if the deacons provide their own chairman, it will be useful to have at least one of the elders present, so that he can express an opinion on any matter that might be deemed more in the area of overseer-responsibility than that of deacon. Furthermore, he will be able to understand and see firsthand and in context any matter which should be tabled for reference to his fellow-overseers.

One other matter might be worthy of mention at this point. It is the importance of bearing in mind the scriptural injunction, "the same commit thou to faithful men, who shall be able to teach others also" (II Tim. 2:2). Whether in the teaching of the Word or the administering of mundane affairs, those who bear responsibility should seek to train others to follow on. Young men should be invited to observe a deacons' meeting so that they might not only gain an insight into the workings of an assembly, but also be prepared to shoulder responsibility intelligently when their turn comes. Many a young man can thank God for a wise, senior brother who encouraged him and gave him opportunities of sharing the yoke. For older men, whether elders or deacons, to reserve all responsibility for themselves or their contemporaries is, to use an old saying, "putting all the eggs in one basket."

THE DEACON'S REWARD

While it is true that the privilege of serving is sufficient reward for the man who serves Christ, Paul indicates that there are additional benefits accruing to faithful deacons. He writes, "For they that have served well as deacons gain to themselves a good standing, and great boldness in the faith which is in Christ Jesus" (I Tim. 3:13). A closer examination of these words will reveal that Paul is not "dangling a carrot," but reiterating a scriptural principle : that service well done brings the reward of added responsibility. Faithful deaconship may enhance a man's reputation, but this simply provides him with a greater challenge and responsibility. This is somewhat reminiscent of the nobleman's commendation in our Lord's parable, "Well done, thou good servant : because thou wast found faithful in a very little, have thou authority over ten cities" (Luke 19:17 RV).

There are two key phrases in these words of Paul to Timothy. First, he says that faithful deacons will *bathmon heautois kalon peripoiountai* (literally, "acquire for themselves a good standing"). Several suggestions are made about the exact meaning of this phrase. One is that it implies that if a deacon does his job well he will "graduate" to the office of an overseer. Now while it may be true practically speaking that deaconship is often a proving ground for eldership, there is no hint here or anywhere else in the text of Scripture that transfer from the role of deacon to that of elder is automatic. An elder's work is quite distinct from that of a deacon, just as are his qualifications. It is quite possible that a man will never engage in other than deacon service.

Another interpretation of this phrase suggests that it refers to the final "standing" of a man before the God whom he has served in the Day of Judgment. Not only does this do despite to the context, but it is theologically unfounded. A man's standing before God depends not on service rendered, but on the precious blood of Christ. This, of course, is not to deny that every Christian, whether deacon, elder, teacher, help or evangelist, will stand before the judgment seat (*bēma*) of Christ to be rewarded for service rendered (I Cor. 3:8, 13-15; 4:5; II Cor. 5:10).

The best interpretation of Paul's phrase is the one that refers it to the deacon's "standing" in the eyes of men, or in the eyes of the local church. This clearly is the emphasis in this particular context, and so patently true. A man who faithfully discharges his mission even if it be in minor matters will quickly come to be respected and held in esteem for his reliability and devotion. He is more likely to be paid the compliment of "being taken for granted," than be congratulated publicly, but nevertheless, he will win a good reputation and this in fact will ultimately widen his field of usefulness. It is well remarked that "influence is a by-product of character." Paul is not advocating that deacons court the praise of men, but observing that diligence will not always pass unnoticed.

The second key phrase in the text under consideration is that a good deacon will have "great boldness (*parrēsia*) in the faith which is in Christ Jesus." The question is raised whether this is "boldness" before God or men. Again the context suggests the latter. Surely it means that the man who serves well wins the right to speak to others. The man whose example is seen is the one whose precept will be followed.

There may also be the idea here that the deacon who has served well and sought to do the will of God will be perfectly relaxed and confident, but this would only be secondary. It is best to understand the concluding phrase "in the faith which is in Christ Jesus" in the sense of "in the Christian faith," which is a characteristic concept in the Pastorals. To sum up, Paul is really saying that the best sermon is the one that is *lived*. Such sermons make an audience receptive. To quote the NEB, "For deacons with a good record of service may claim a high standing and the right to speak openly on matters of the Christian faith."

DEACONS AND THEIR SUFFICIENCY

As we conclude this section concerning the ministry of deacons, it may be well to re-emphasize that it is Christ-honouring service that counts, not the securing of social or ecclesiastical preferment. Happy the man who, whatever his sphere, has "done what he could," for there is no doubt that he will hear his Lord say, "Well done!"

A BIBLIOGRAPHY

Abbott Smith, G. A.	A Manual Greek Lexicon of the New Testament	T. and T. Clark, 1948
Allen, Roland	The Spontaneous Expansion of the Church	
Blackwood, A. W.	Pastoral Leadership	Abingdon-Cokesbury
Blaiklock, E. M.	The Acts of the Apostles (TNTC)	Tyndale Press, 1959
Barclay, William	The Letters to Timothy, Titus and Philemon.	St. Andrew's Press, 1962
Borlase, Henry	Reasons for Withdrawing from the Ministry of the Established Church	1834
Broadbent, E. H.	The Pilgrim Church	Pickering and Inglis, 1950
Bruce, F. F.	The Acts of the Apostles (Greek Text)	Tyndale Press, 1951
Bruce, F. F.	The Book of Acts (NLCNT)	Marshall, Morgan and Scott, 1954
Bruce, F. F.	The Spreading Flame	The Paternoster Press, 1971
Bruce, F. F.	The Epistle to the Ephesians	Pickering and Inglis, 1961
Bruce, F. F.	The English Bible	Lutterworth Press, 1961
Brunner, Emil	The Misunderstanding of the Church	
Coad, F. R.	A History of the Brethren Movement	The Paternoster Press, 1968
Conybeare and Howson	The Life and Epistles of St. Paul	Longmans, 1905

141

Craik, Henry	New Testament Church Order	1863
Craik, Henry	The Authority of Scripture Considered in Relation to Christian Union	1863
Darby, J. N.	Collected Writings	
Guthrie, Motyer, Stibbs, Wiseman (Eds.)	The New Bible Commentary (Revd.)	Inter-Varsity Press, 1955
Douglas, J. D. (Ed.)	The New Bible Dictionary	Inter-Varsity Press, 1962
Ellison, H. L.	The Household Church	The Paternoster Press, 1963
Godet, F.	Epistle to the Romans	T. and T. Clark, 1889
Gosse, E.	Father and Son	
Guthrie, D. M.	The Pastoral Epistles (TNTC)	Tyndale Press, 1959
Hatch, Edwin	The Organization of the Early Christian Churches	
(High Leigh)	A New Testament Church in 1955. A Return to Simplicity	Conference Reports, 1955, 1956
Holmes, Frank	Brother Indeed	Victory Press, 1956
Hort, F. J. A.	The Christian Ekklesia	
Ironside, H. A.	A Historical Sketch of the Brethren Movement	1941
Jowett, J. H.	The Preacher; his Life and Work	Hodder and Stoughton
Kelly, W.	Lectures on the Church of God	
Kirby, Gilbert	The Protestant Churches of Britain	
Lang, G. H.	The Churches of God	The Paternoster Press, 1959
Lang, G. H.	Anthony Norris Groves	The Paternoster Press
Lang, G. H.	God at Work on His Own Lines	1952
Lightfoot, J. B.	St. Paul's Epistle to the Philippians	Macmillan, 1898

Lindsay, T. M.	The Church and the Ministry in the Early Church	
Lloyd-Jones, D. M.	The Basis of Christian Unity	Tyndale Press, 1963
Macdonald, William	Christ Loved the Church	Emmaus Bible School (Correspondence Course)
Morris, Leon	I and II Thessalonians (TNTC)	Tyndale Press, 1963
Muller, G.	A Narrative of some of the Lord's Dealings with George Muller	1881
Murray, Iain (ed.)	The Reformation of the Church	
Neatby, W. B.	A History of the Plymouth Brethren	1901
Pickering, H.	Great Men among the Brethren	
Pierson, A. T.	George Müller of Bristol	Nisbet, 1900
Pollock, J. C.	Hudson Taylor and Maria	Hodder & Stoughton, 1962
Rowdon, H.	The Origins of the Brethren	Pickering & Inglis, 1967
Sangster, W. E.	The Approach to Preaching	Epworth Press 1951
Simpson, E. K.	The Pastoral Epistles	Tyndale Press, 1954
Soltau, H. W.	The Tabernacle, the Priesthood and the Offerings	
Souter, Alexander	Novum Testamentum Graece	Oxford University Press, 1962
Stibbs, A.	God's Church	Inter-Varsity Press, 1959
Surridge, F. W.	The Finest of the Wheat	1950
Trotter, W. (Mrs.)	Undertones of the Nineteenth Century	1905

Vine, W. E.	An Expository Dictionary of New Testament Words	Oliphants, 1946
Vine, W. E.	The Church and the Churches	John Ritchie
Watson, J. B. (Ed.)	The Church: a Symposium	Pickering and Inglis, 1952
Westcott, B. F.	Epistle to the Ephesians	Macmillan, 1906

Magazines:

The Harvester	The Paternoster Press, Exeter
The Witness	Pickering and Inglis, Ltd., Glasgow
Interest	Stewards Foundation Inc., Wheaton, Ill.
The Believer's Magazine	John Ritchie, Ltd., (Kilmarnock)
Echoes of Service	Echoes of Service, Bath
The Fields	The Fields, Inc., (New York)